THIS BOOK BELONGS TO

QUILT DESIGNS
IN CROSS-STITCH

QUILT DESIGNS
IN CROSS-STITCH

By The Vanessa-Ann Collection

Sedgewood® Press
New York, N.Y.

For Sedgewood® Press
Director: ELIZABETH P. RICE
Manager, Product Development:
    PATRICIA VAN NOTE
Production Manager: BILL ROSE

For the Vanessa-Ann Collection
Owners: JO PACKHAM and
        TERRECE BEESLEY WOODRUFF

Staff: KATHI ALLRED
    GLORIA BAUR
    VICKI BURKE
    CHRISTINE DEETER
    KRISTEN JARCHOW
    SUSAN JORGENSEN
    MARGARET MARTI
    BARBARA MILBURN
    PAMELA RANDALL
    JULIE TRUMAN
    NANCY WHITLEY

Designers: TRICE BOERENS
        MARY CALE
        JO PACKHAM
        JULIE TRUMAN
        TERRECE WOODRUFF

Photographer: RYNE HAZEN

ISBN: 0-696-02321-0
First Printing 1989
Library of Congress Catalog number: 88-063216

Published by Sedgewood® Press

Distributed by Meredith Corporation,
Des Moines, Iowa.

10 9 8 7 6 5 4 3 2 1

To Sara and Justin,
Thank you for helping to make all of my dreams come true.

I love you,
Mom

Much of the photography for this book was done at Mary Gaskill's Trends and Traditions, part of Historic 25th Street, Ogden, Utah. Other photographs were taken in the homes of Susan Whitelock, Ogden, Utah, and Edie Stockstill, Salt Lake City, Utah.

The Vanessa-Ann Collection expresses its thanks for their cooperation.

CONTENTS

Stitch Count: 136 × 195

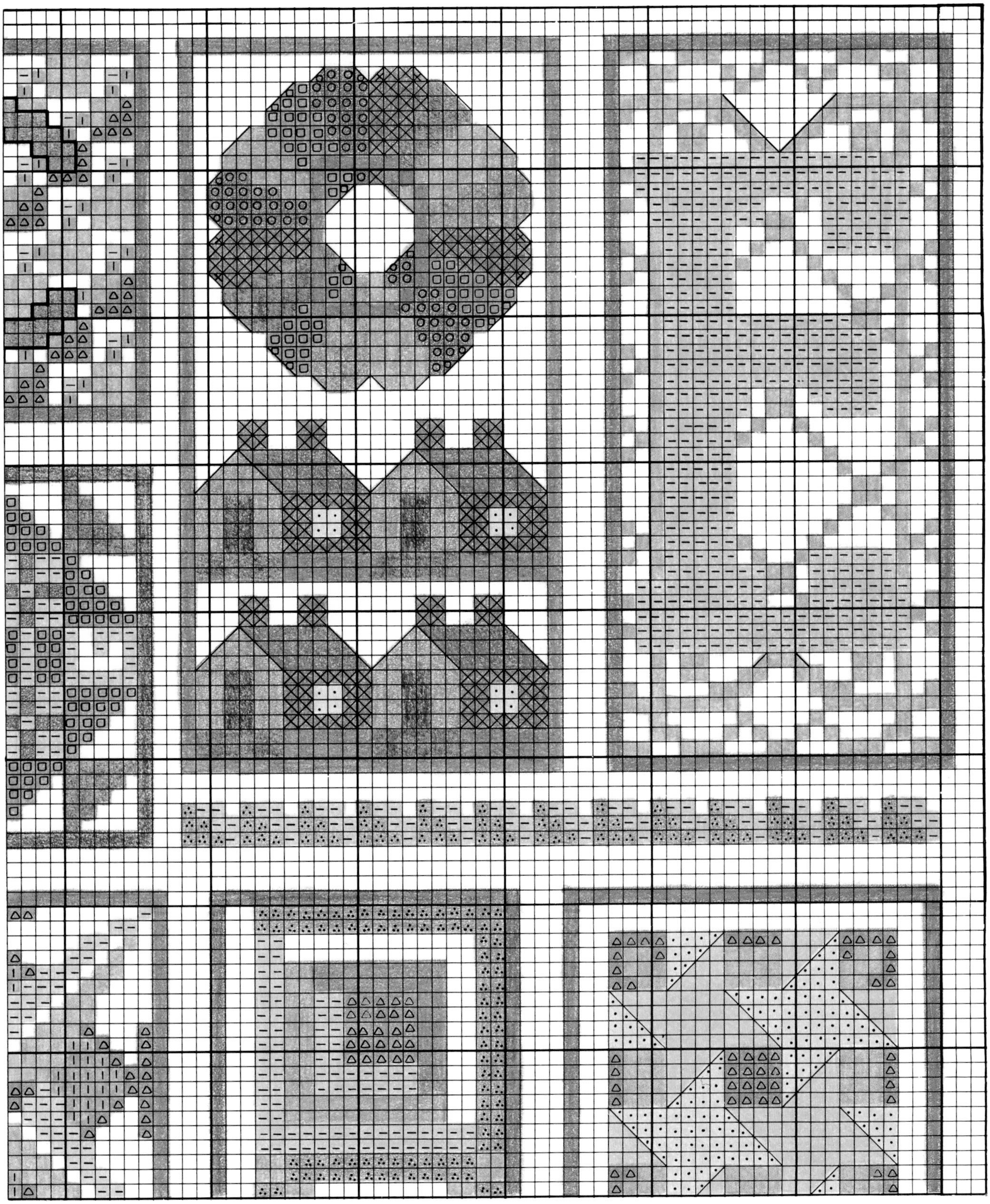

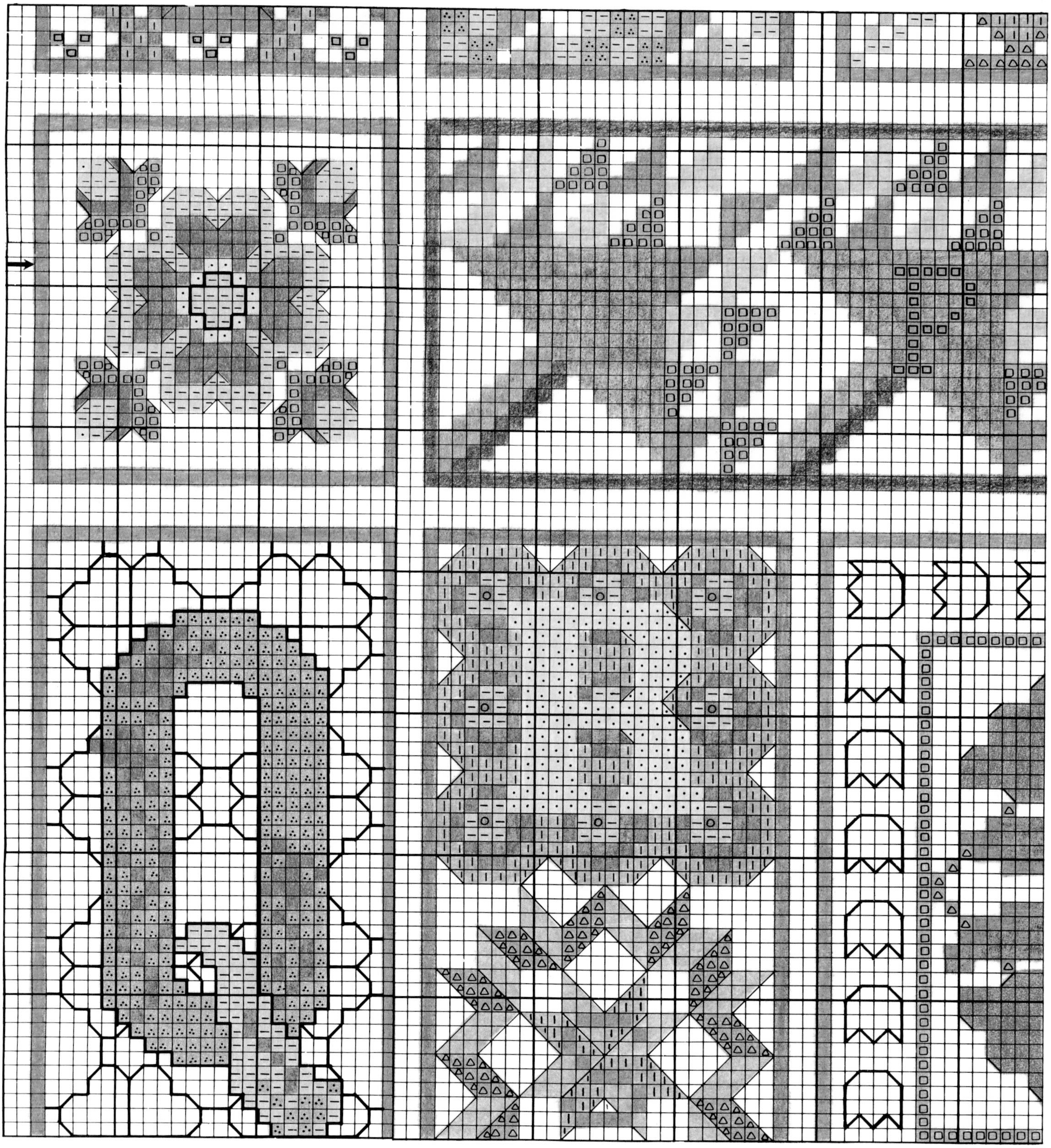

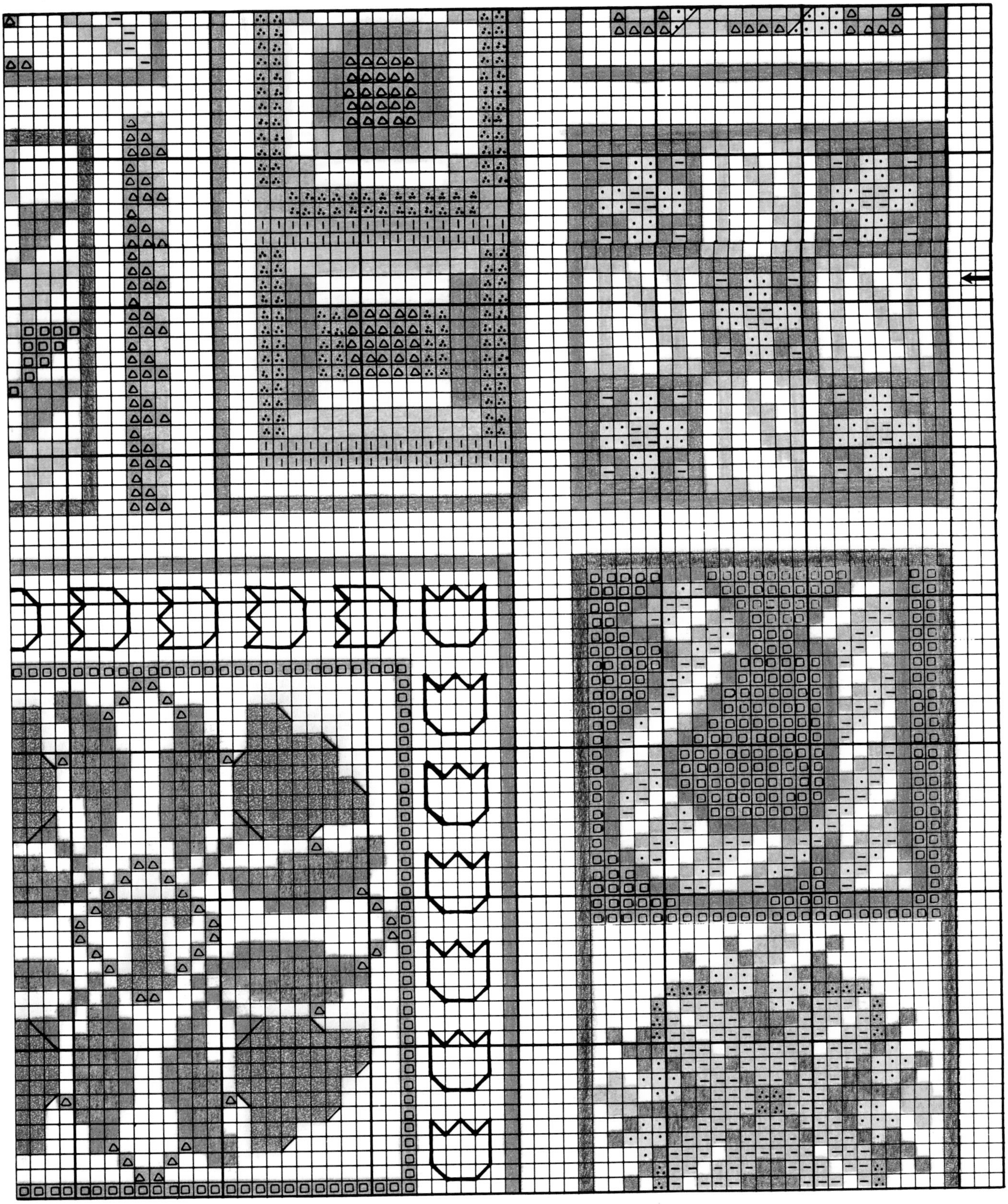

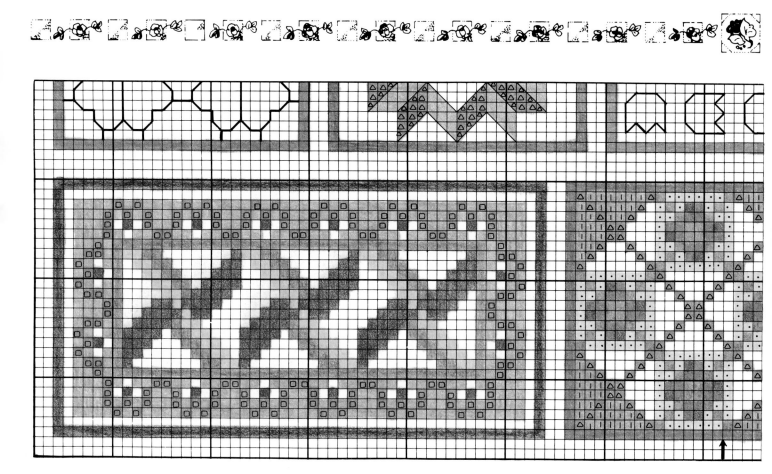

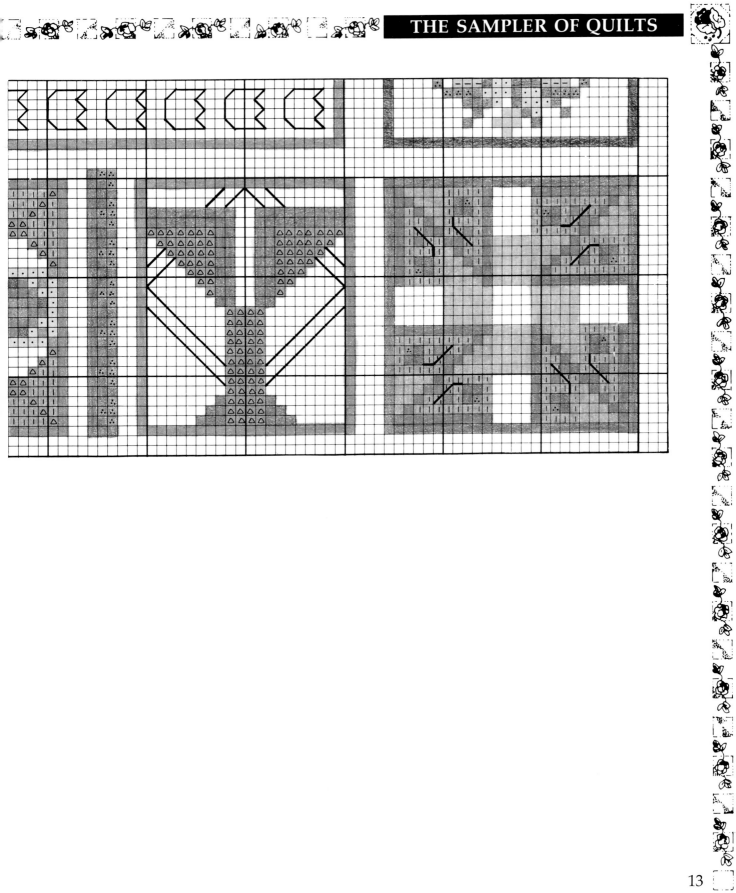

SAMPLE

Stiched on Cream Belfast Linen 32 over two threads, the finished design size is 8½" × 12¼". The fabric was cut 15" × 19".

FABRIC	DESIGN SIZES
Aida 11	12⅜" × 17¾"
Aida 14	9¾" × 13⅞"
Aida 18	7½" × 10⅞"
Hardanger 22	6⅛" × 8⅞"

ANCHOR			DMC (used for sample)	

Step One: Cross-stitch (two strands)

891	676 Old Gold-lt.
890	729 Old Gold-med.
8	761 Salmon-lt.
9	760 Salmon
11	3328 Salmon-med.
13	347 Salmon-dk.
22	816 Garnet
43	815 Garnet-med.
869	3042 Antique Violet-lt.
871	3041 Antique Violet-med.
920	932 Antique Blue-lt.
921	931 Antique Blue-med.
922	930 Antique Blue-dk.
875	503 Blue Green-med.
876	502 Blue Green
878	501 Blue Green-dk.
214	368 Pistachio Green-lt.
215	320 Pistachio Green-med.
843	3364 Pine Green
309	435 Brown-vy. lt.
349	301 Mahogany-med.
352	300 Mahogany-vy. dk.

Step Two: Backstitch (one strand)

43	815 Garnet-med. (block with letter "O")
878	501 Blue Green-dk. (all else)

Step Three: Feather stitch (one strand)

871	3041 Antique Violet-med.

SAMPLE - FOUR MINIATURE BLOCKS

Stitched on Silk Canvas 30 over one thread, the finished design size is ⅞" × ⅞". The fabric was cut 3" × 3".

FABRIC	DESIGN SIZES
Aida 11	2⅜" × 2⅜"
Aida 14	1⅞" × 1⅞"
Aida 18	1½" × 1½"
Hardanger 22	1⅛" × 1⅛"

Stitch Count: 26 × 26

SAMPLE - A PATCHWORK JEWELRY BOX

Stitched on Cream Belfast Linen 32 over two threads, the finished design size is 3⅛" × 3⅛". The fabric was cut 8" × 8".

FABRIC	DESIGN SIZES
Aida 11	4½" × 4½"
Aida 14	3⅝" × 3⅝"
Aida 18	2¾" × 2¾"
Hardanger 22	2¼" × 2¼"

Stitch Count: 50 × 50

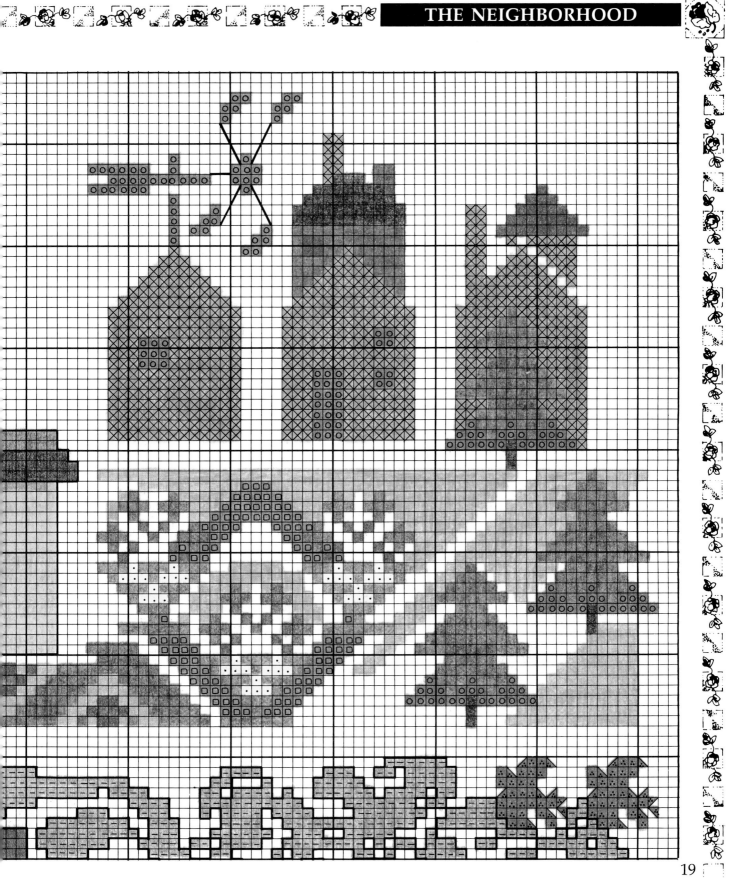

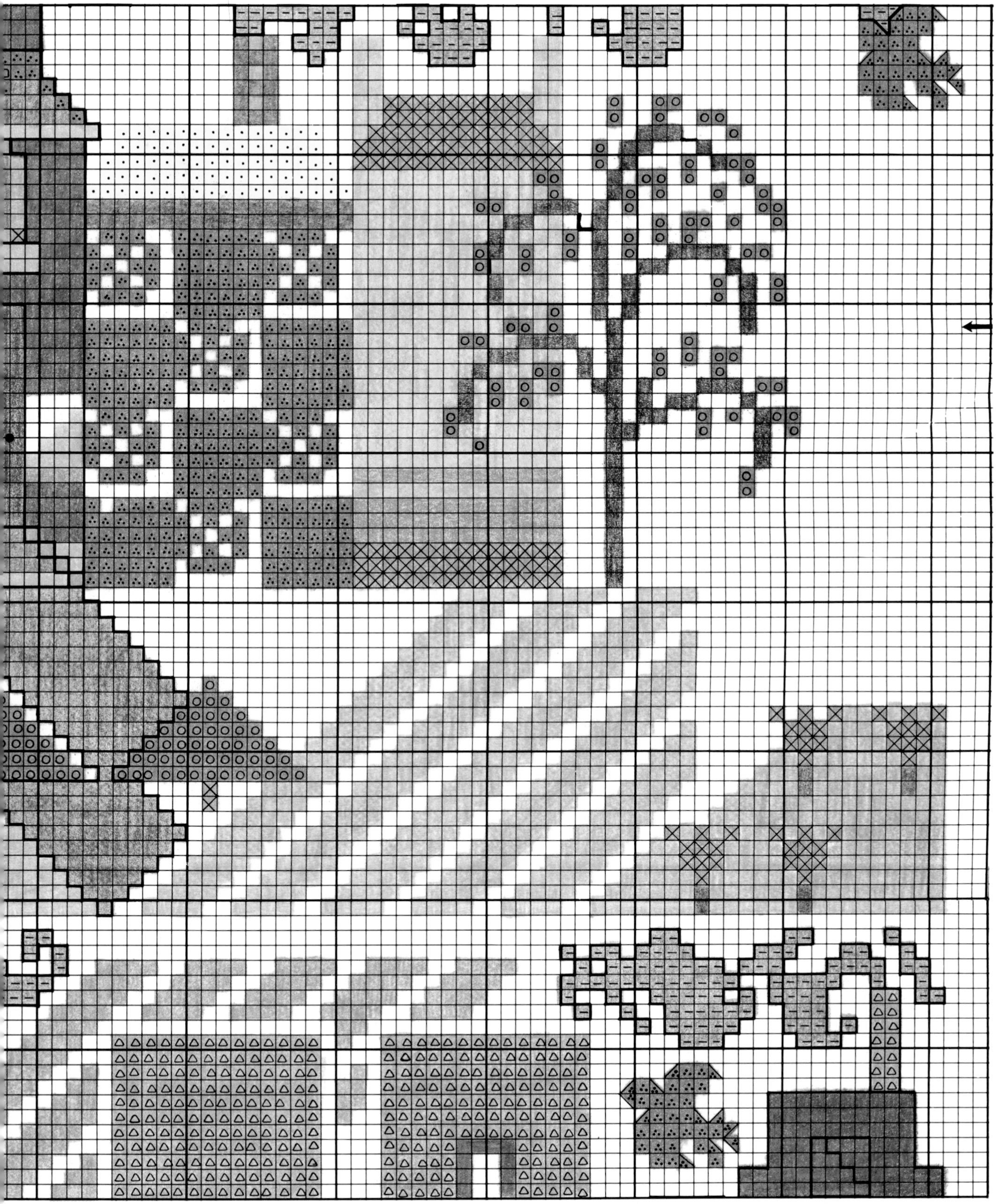

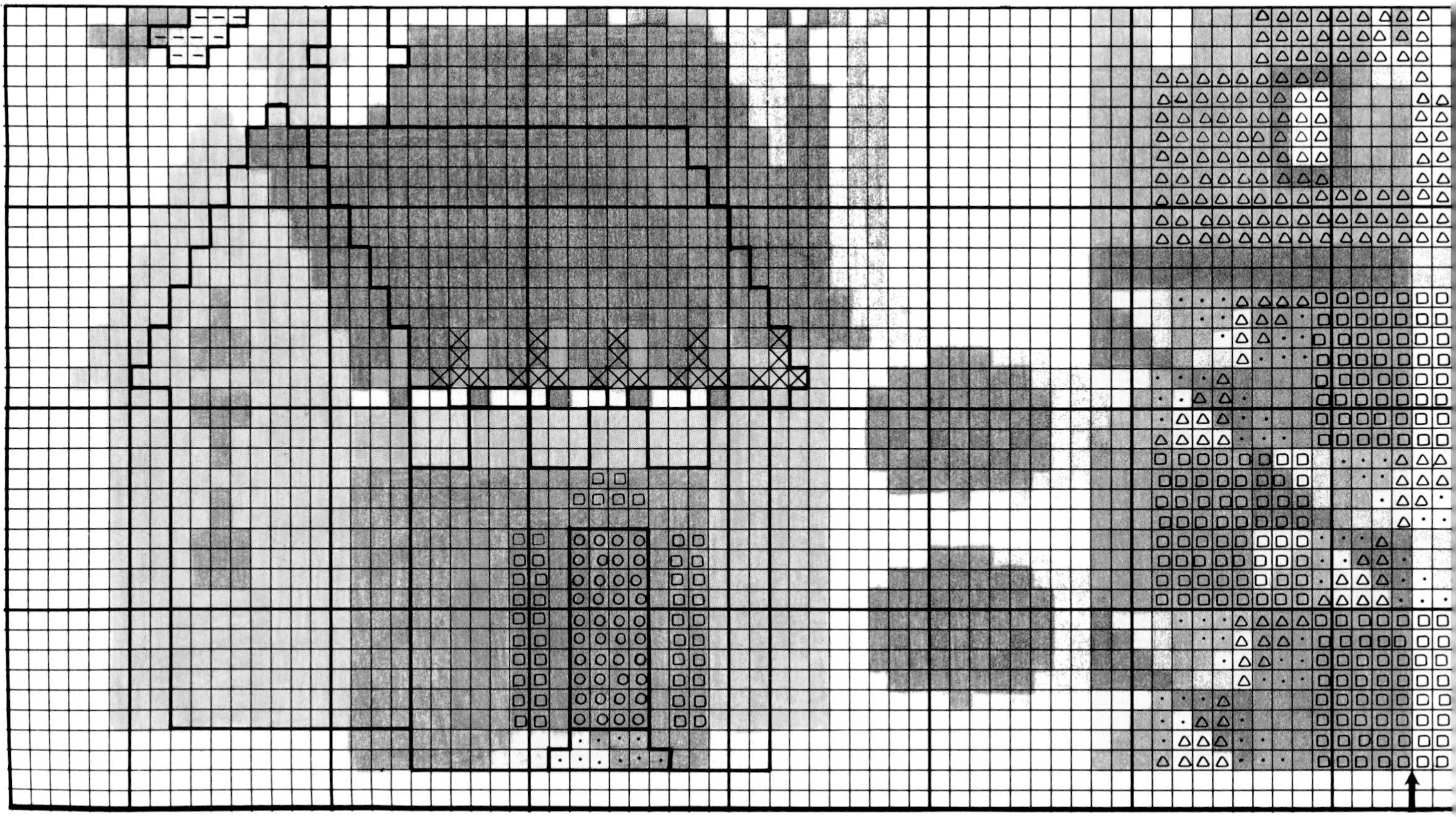

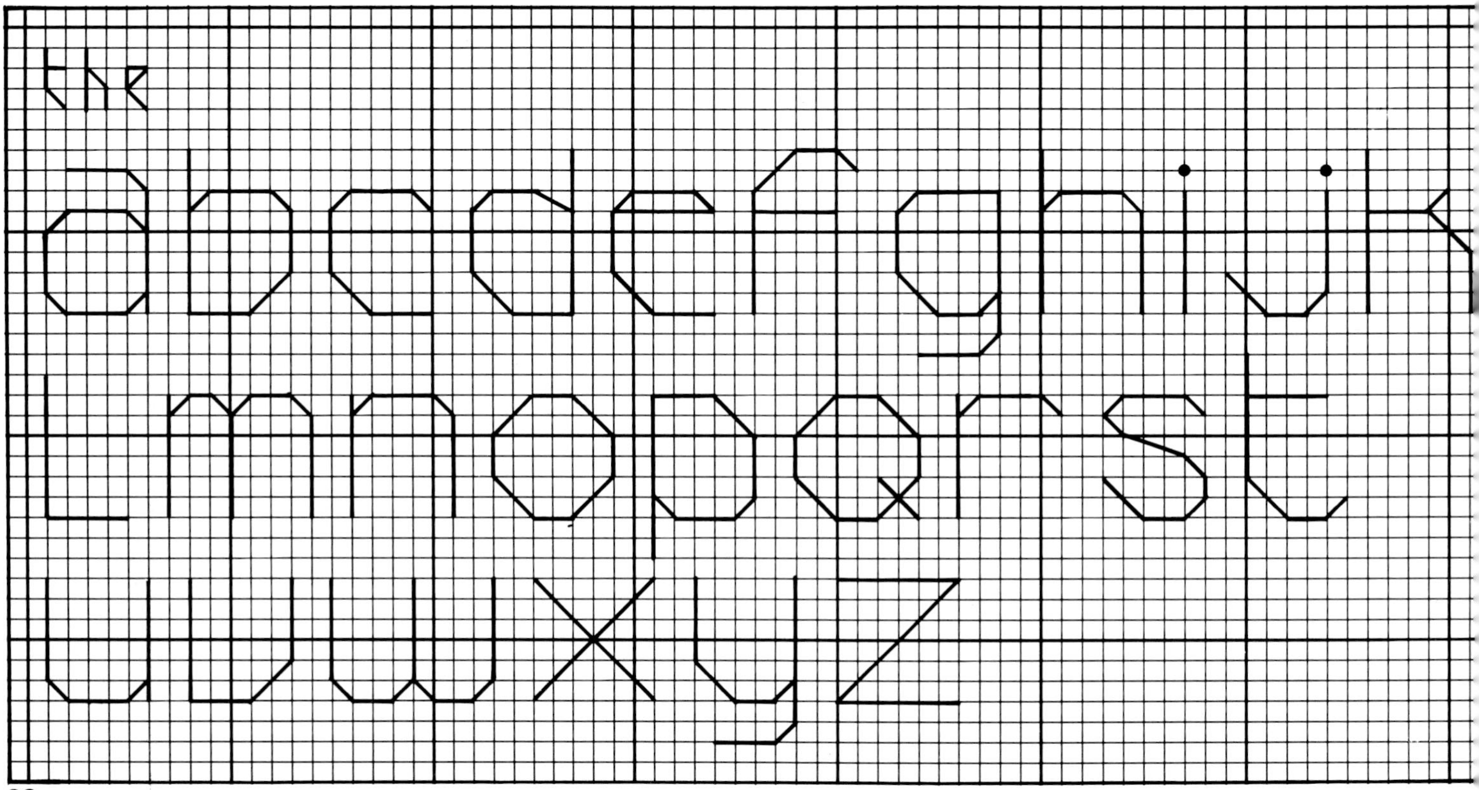
the
abcdefghijk
lmnopqrst
uvwxyz

SAMPLE

Stitched on Pewter Jobelan 28 over two threads, the finished design size is 9¾" × 13¾". The fabric was cut 16" × 20".

FABRIC	DESIGN SIZES
Aida 11	12⅜" × 17½"
Aida 14	9¾" × 13¾"
Aida 18	7½" × 10¾"
Hardanger 22	6⅛" × 8¾"

ANCHOR   **DMC** (used for sample)

Step One: Cross-stitch (two strands)

886	677 Old Gold-vy. lt.
868	758 Terra Cotta-lt.
882	407 Sportsman Flesh-dk.
968	778 Antique Mauve-lt.
74	3354 Dusty Rose-lt.
894	223 Shell Pink-med.
897	221 Shell Pink-dk.
869	3042 Antique Violet-lt.
871	3041 Antique Violet-med.
101	327 Antique Violet-dk.
120	794 Cornflower Blue-lt.
145	334 Baby Blue-med.

978	322 Navy Blue-vy. lt.
920	932 Antique Blue-lt.
849	927 Slate Green-med.
167	598 Turquoise-lt.
213	504 Blue Green-lt.
876	502 Blue Green
878	501 Blue Green-dk.
378	841 Beige Brown-lt.
379	840 Beige Brown-med.
397	762 Pearl Gray-vy. lt.

Step Two: Backstitch (one strand)

1	White (clouds)
101	327 Antique Violet-dk. (windows in pink house)
878	501 Blue Green-dk. (weather vane)
379	840 Beige Brown-med. (tree branches and baskets in window)
862	934 Black Avocado Green (all else)

Step Three: French Knots (one strand)

862	934 Black Avocado Green

23

SAMPLE - THE FAMILY SAMPLER

Stitched on Pewter Jobelan 28 over two threads, the finished design size is 9⅝" × 5¾". The fabric was cut 16" × 12".

Begin stitching the bottom edge of the sampler (see photo) 3" above the bottom edge of the fabric, centering the design horizontally. To personalize the sampler, transfer the letters to graph paper. Mark the horizontal center of the graph and, on the fabric, mark a straight line ⅝" above the first rooftop. Center the name horizontally above the line.

FABRIC	DESIGN SIZES
Aida 11	12⅛" × 7¼"
Aida 14	9⅝" × 5¾"
Aida 18	7½" × 4½"
Hardanger 22	1⅛" × 3⅝"

Stitch Count: 134 × 80

24

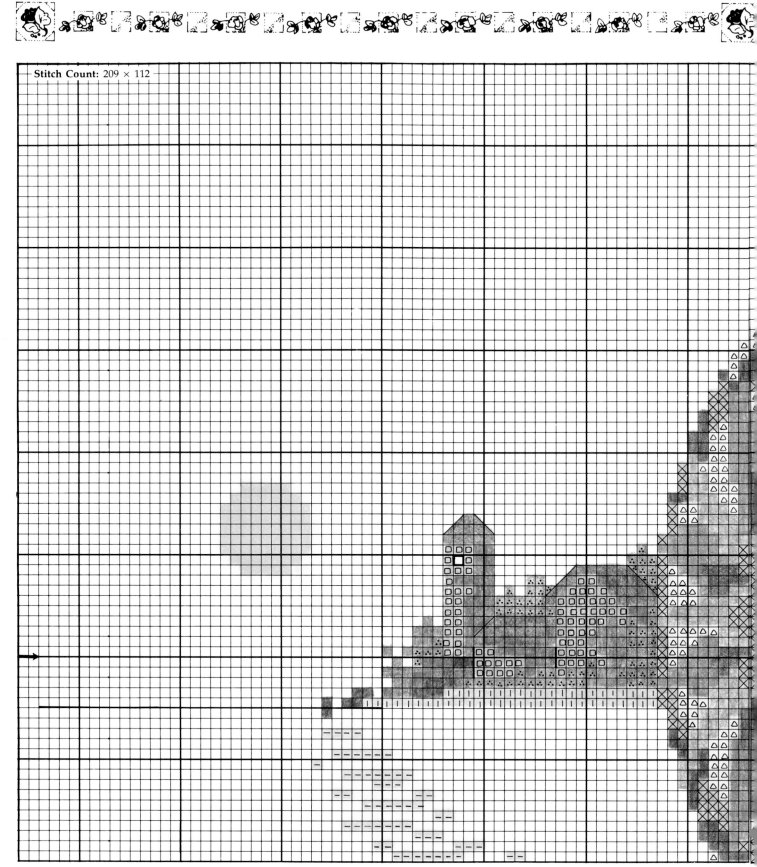

Stitch Count: 209 × 112

Continued on page 31.

Continued on page 30.

Continued on page 32.

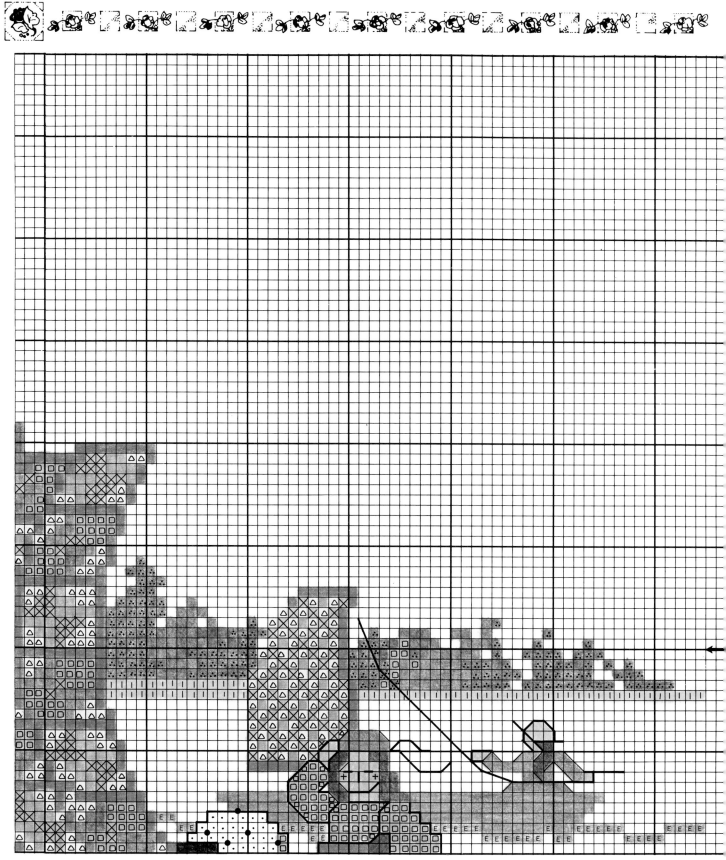

Continued on page 33.

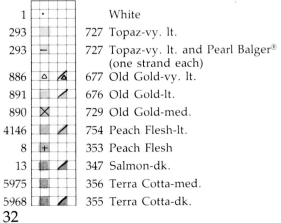

SAMPLE

Stitched on Blue Glenshee Linen 29 over two threads, the finished design size is 14½" × 7¾". The fabric was cut 21" × 14".

FABRIC	DESIGN SIZES
Aida 11	19" × 10⅛"
Aida 14	14⅞" × 8"
Aida 18	11⅝" × 6¼"
Hardanger 22	9½" × 5⅛"

ANCHOR   **DMC** (used for sample)

Step One: Cross-stitch (two strands)

ANCHOR		DMC	
1	·		White
293		727	Topaz-vy. lt.
293	−	727	Topaz-vy. lt. and Pearl Balger® (one strand each)
886	△ ◢	677	Old Gold-vy. lt.
891	◢	676	Old Gold-lt.
890	☒	729	Old Gold-med.
4146	◢	754	Peach Flesh-lt.
8	+	353	Peach Flesh
13	◢	347	Salmon-dk.
5975		356	Terra Cotta-med.
5968	◢	355	Terra Cotta-dk.

159		3325	Baby Blue
159	E	3325	Baby Blue and Pearl Balger® (one strand each)
167		597	Turquoise
168	◢	518	Wedgewood-lt.
164	◢	824	Blue-vy. dk.
843		3364	Pine Green
876	⠿ ◢	502	Blue Green
246		319	Pistachio Green-vy. dk.
942	I	738	Tan-vy. lt.
347		402	Mahogany-vy. lt.
349	◢	301	Mahogany-med.
352	○	300	Mahogany-vy. dk.
371		433	Brown-med.
357		801	Coffee Brown-dk.
382	◢	3371	Black Brown
397	○ ◢	762	Pearl Gray-vy. lt.
398		415	Pearl Gray
8581		646	Beaver Gray-dk.

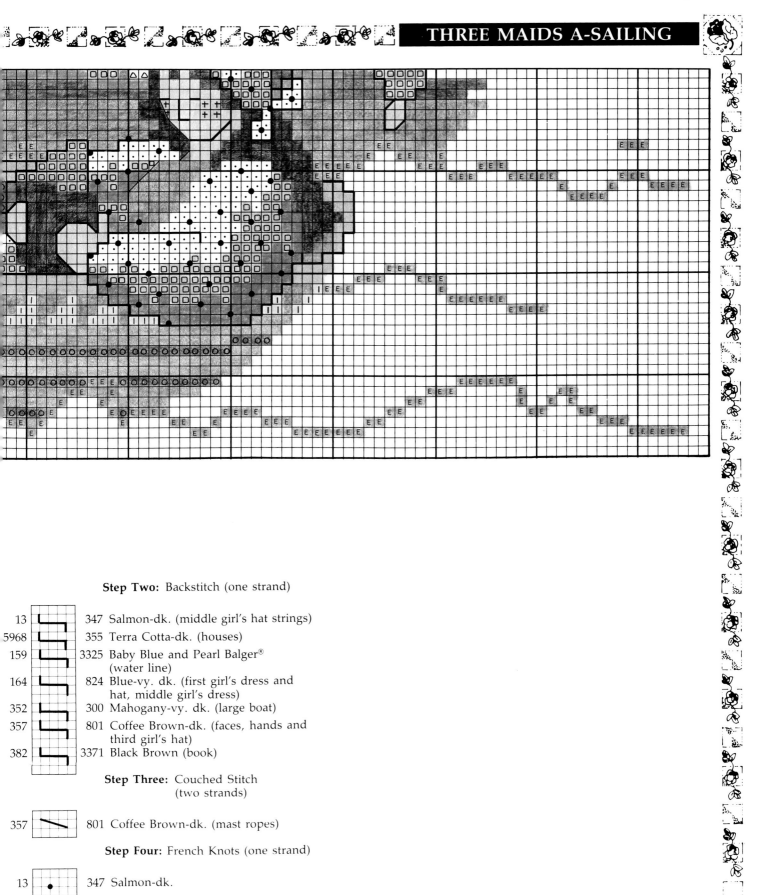

Step Two: Backstitch (one strand)

13	347	Salmon-dk. (middle girl's hat strings)
5968	355	Terra Cotta-dk. (houses)
159	3325	Baby Blue and Pearl Balger® (water line)
164	824	Blue-vy. dk. (first girl's dress and hat, middle girl's dress)
352	300	Mahogany-vy. dk. (large boat)
357	801	Coffee Brown-dk. (faces, hands and third girl's hat)
382	3371	Black Brown (book)

Step Three: Couched Stitch
(two strands)

357	801	Coffee Brown-dk. (mast ropes)

Step Four: French Knots (one strand)

13	347	Salmon-dk.

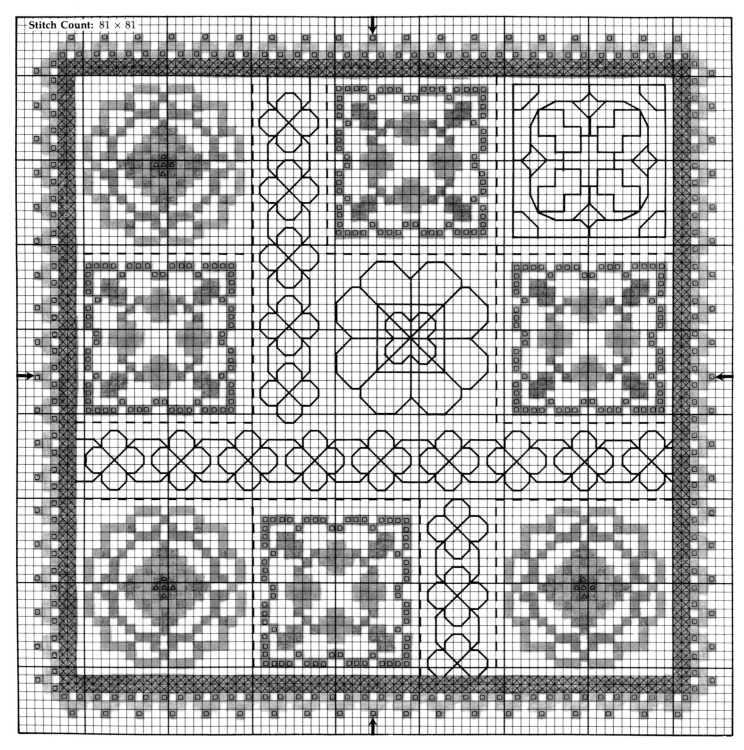

Stitch Count: 81 × 81

SAMPLE – A MAIDEN'S MOSAIC

Stitched on Cream Hardanger 22 over two threads, the finished design size is 7⅜″ × 7⅜″. The fabric was cut 14″ × 14″.

FABRIC	DESIGN SIZES
Aida 11	7⅜″ × 7⅜″
Aida 14	5¾″ × 5¾″
Aida 18	4½″ × 4½″
Hardanger 22	3⅝″ × 3⅝″

ANCHOR   **DMC** (used for sample)

Step One: Cross-stitch (two strands)

74		3354 Dusty Rose-lt.
69		3687 Mauve
869		3042 Antique Violet-lt.
871	△	3041 Antique Violet-med.
167		597 Turquoise
168	▢	518 Wedgewood-lt.
164	✕	824 Blue-vy. dk.
876		502 Blue Green

Step Two: Backstitch (one strand)

164		824 Blue-vy. dk.

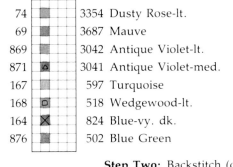

SAMPLE – NAVIGATOR'S BOX TABLE

Stitched on cream Hardanger 22 over two threads, the finished design size is 11⅛″ × 8⅛″. The fabric was cut 16″ × 13″.

FABRIC	DESIGN SIZES
Aida 11	11⅛″ × 8⅛″
Aida 14	8¾″ × 6⅜″
Aida 18	6¾″ × 5″
Hardanger 22	5½″ × 4⅛″

ANCHOR **DMC** (used for sample)

Step One: Cross-stitch (three strands)

ANCHOR		DMC	
886		677	Old Gold-vy. lt.
8		353	Peach Flesh
74	✕	3354	Dusty Rose-lt.
69		3687	Mauve
869		3042	Antique Violet-lt.
871		3041	Antique Violet-med.
158	·	747	Sky Blue-vy. lt.
159		3325	Baby Blue
161	○	826	Blue-med.
164		824	Blue-vy. dk.
167		597	Turquoise
168	△	518	Wedgewood-lt.
876		502	Blue Green
246		319	Pistachio Green-vy. dk.

Step Two: Backstitch (one strand)

74		3354 Dusty Rose-lt.

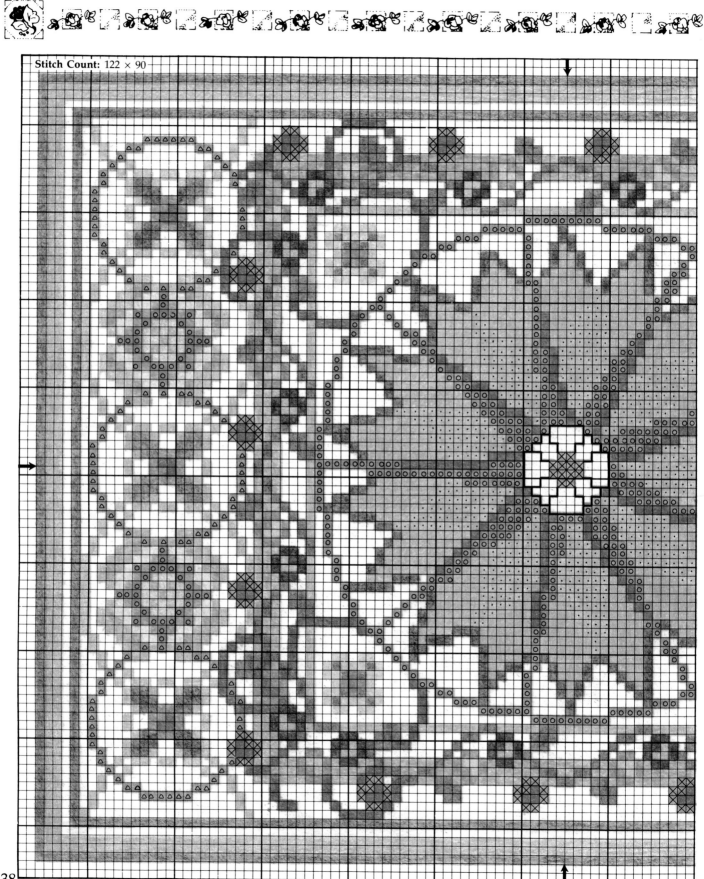

Stitch Count: 122 × 90

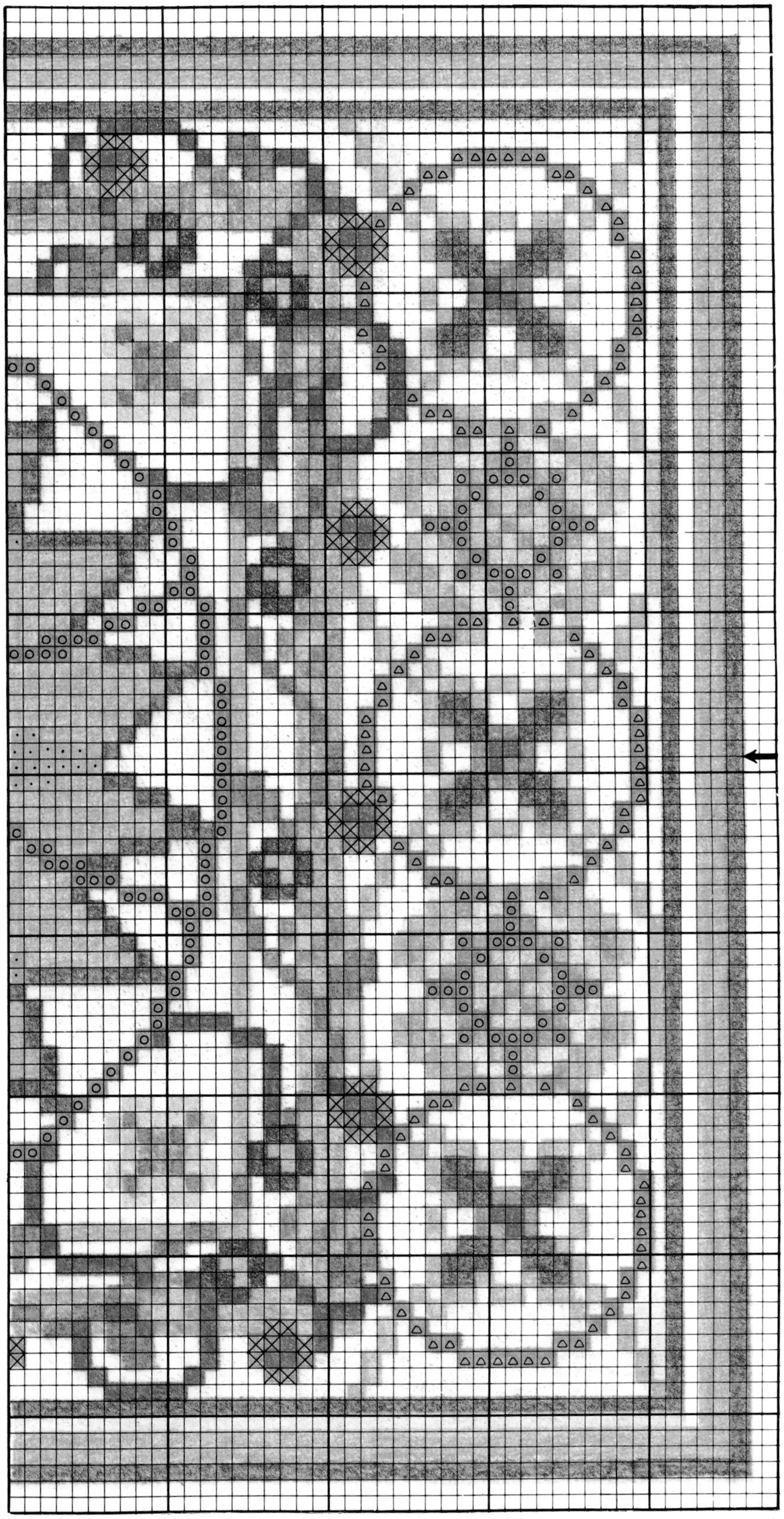

Stitch Count: 137 x 183

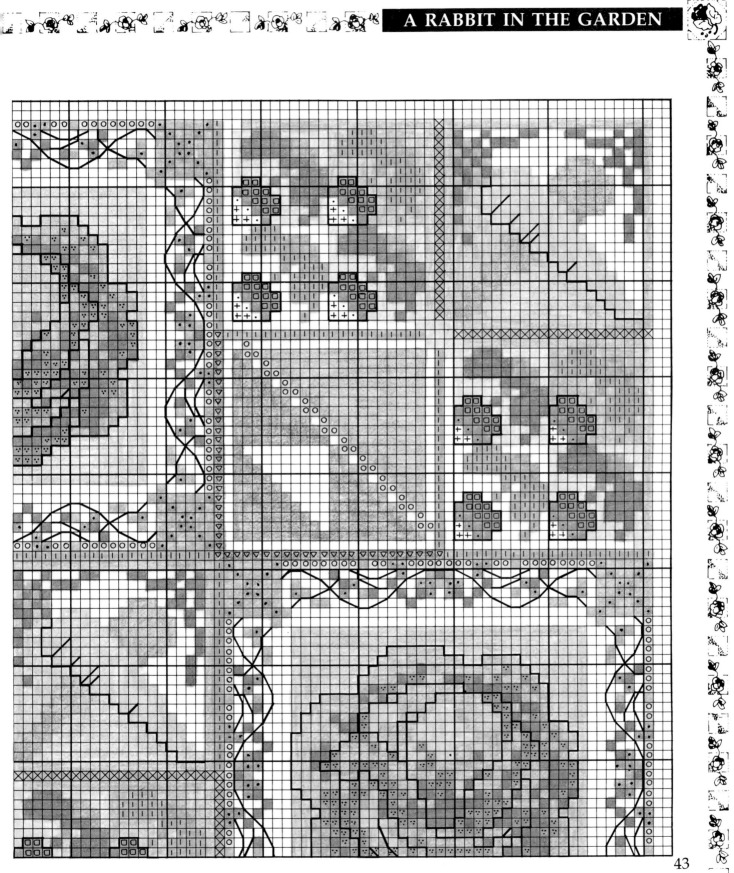

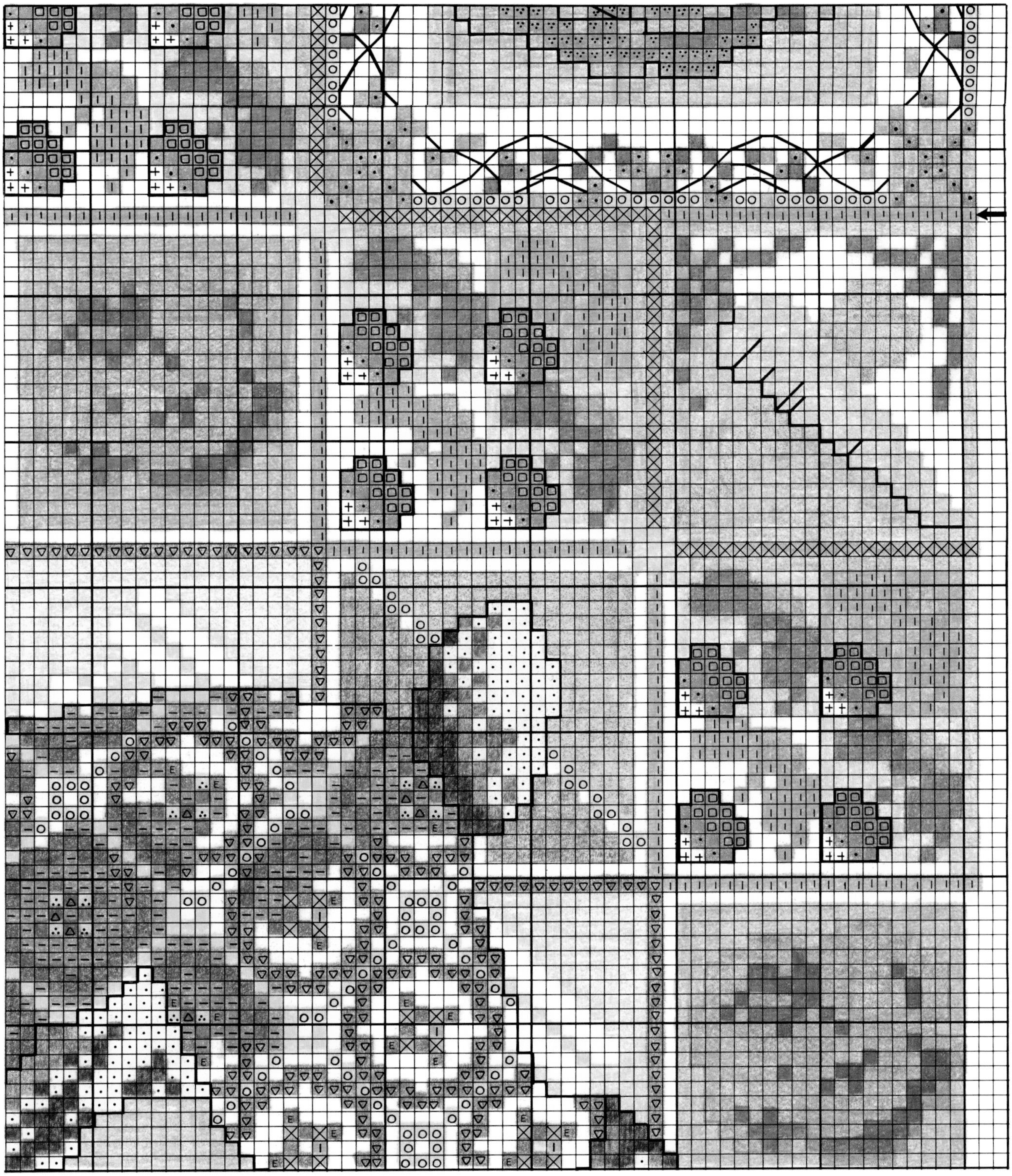

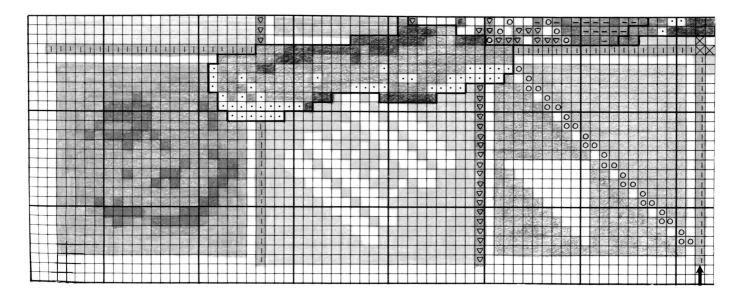

SAMPLE

Stitched on White Belfast Linen 32 over two threads, the finished design size is 8½″ × 11½″. The fabric was cut 15″ × 18″.

FABRIC	DESIGN SIZES
Aida 11	12½″ × 16⅝″
Aida 14	9¾″ × 13⅛″
Aida 18	7⅝″ × 10⅛″
Hardanger 22	6¼″ × 8⅜″

ANCHOR　　**DMC** (used for sample)

Step One: Cross-stitch (two strands)

1	+	White
386	· /	746 Off White
886	o	677 Old Gold-vy. lt.
886		677 Old Gold-vy. lt. (one strand)
306		725 Topaz
8	∴	353 Peach Flesh
868		758 Terra Cotta-lt.
882		407 Sportsman Flesh-dk.
892	✕	225 Shell Pink-vy. lt.
892		225 Shell Pink-vy. lt. (one strand)
893	▢	224 Shell Pink-lt.
894		223 Shell Pink-med.
968		778 Antique Mauve-lt. (one strand)
968	•	778 Antique Mauve-lt.

49	▬	3689 Mauve-lt.
66		3688 Mauve-med.
69	△	3687 Mauve
869		3042 Antique Violet-lt.
871		3041 Antique Violet-med.
117	E	341 Blue Violet-lt.
118		340 Blue Violet-med.
167		598 Turquoise-lt.
920	▽	932 Antique Blue-lt.
920		932 Antique Blue-lt. (one strand)
145		334 Baby Blue-med.
206		369 Pistachio Green-vy. lt.
214		368 Pistachio Green-lt.
213	I	504 Blue Green-lt.
213		504 Blue Green-lt. (one strand)
875	⠭	503 Blue Green-med.
876		502 Blue Green
363		436 Tan
370		434 Brown-lt.
401	╱	844 Beaver Gray-ultra dk.

Step Two: Backstitch (one strand)

894		223 Shell Pink-med. (radishes)
878		501 Blue Green-dk. (carrots, lettuce and vines)
401		844 Beaver Gray-ultra dk. (rabbit)

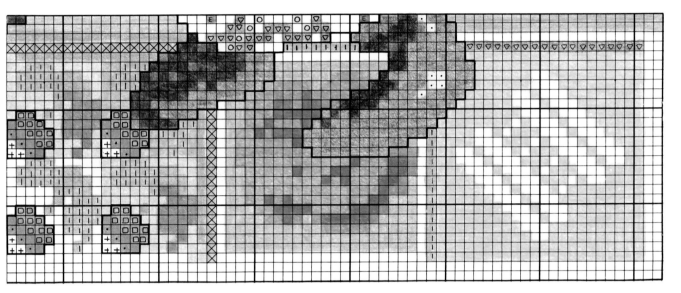

SAMPLE - BREAD BASKET LINER

Stitched on White Belfast Linen 32 over two threads, the finished design size for the radish, cabbage and carrot motifs is 1½" × 1½". The finished design size for the lettuce motif is 2¾" × 2¾". The fabric was cut 18" × 18". Stitch the first lettuce motif in each corner 1½" from the edge. Continue pattern with radish, cabbage and carrot motifs 1" apart on each edge.

FABRIC	Lettuce Motif DESIGN SIZES	Other Motifs DESIGN SIZES
Aida 11	4⅛" × 4⅛"	2⅛" × 2⅛"
Aida 14	3¼" × 3¼"	1¾" × 1¾"
Aida 18	2½" × 2½"	1⅜" × 1⅜"
Hardanger 22	2" × 2"	1⅛" × 1⅛"

Stitch Count: 45 × 45 **Stitch Count:** 24 × 24

MATERIALS

Completed cross-stitch on white Belfast Linen 32; matching thread

DIRECTIONS

1. Trim Linen to 18" square. Stitch with a narrow zig-zag stitch 1" from edge.
2. Fray all edges to edge of zig-zag stitch.

SAMPLE - JAR LID COVERS

Stitched on White Belfast Linen 32 over two threads, the finished design size for each motif is 1½" × 1½". The fabric was cut 9" × 9" for the cabbage and carrot motifs and 10" × 10" for radish motifs. For cabbage and carrot motifs, stitch one motif in center of each cover. For radish motif, stitch the one motif in each corner 1½" from the edge.

FABRIC	DESIGN SIZES
Aida 11	2⅛" × 2⅛"
Aida 14	1¾" × 1¾"
Aida 18	1⅜" × 1⅜"
Hardanger 22	1⅛" × 1⅛"

Stitch Count: 24 × 24

MATERIALS

Completed cross-stitch on White Belfast Linen 32; matching thread

DIRECTIONS

1. Stitch with a narrow zig-zag stitch 1" from edge.
2. Fray all edges to edge of zig-zag stitch.

SAMPLE - A DECORATIVE SHELF LINER

Stitched on White Belfast Linen 32 over two threads, the finished design size for one lettuce motif is 2¾" × 2¾". Cut the fabric the length of the shelf plus 2" by the width of the shelf plus 6". Mark the center of one long edge. Center and stitch the first motif 1" from the edge. Allow 3¼" between motifs. Stitch as many repeats of the motif as needed.

FABRIC	DESIGN SIZES
Aida 11	4⅛" × 4⅛"
Aida 14	3¼" × 3¼"
Aida 18	2½" × 2½"
Hardanger 22	2" × 2"

Stitch Count: 45 × 45

MATERIALS

Completed cross-stitch on white Linen 32; (see sample information); matching thread
Dressmaker's pen

DIRECTIONS

1. Make a 2½" × 3" template. Mark hemline ½" below edge of design. Then center and trace template between motifs with bottom edge on hemline.

2. Cut ¼" outside pen lines. Zig-zag or serge all edges. Clip inside corners. Fold under ¼" and slip-stitch to shelf liner. Starch and iron before using.

SAMPLE - A GARDENER'S HAND TOWEL

Stitched on White Belfast Linen 32 over two threads, the complete finished design size is 21" × 1½". The fabric was cut 32" × 24". One motif consists of the radish square and the carrot square stitched side-by-side. The finished size for one motif is 3" × 1½". Begin stitching in the center 4" from one 24" edge and repeat the motif seven times.

FABRIC	One Motif DESIGN SIZES	Complete Design DESIGN SIZES
Aida 11	4⅜" × 4½"	30½" × 4½"
Aida 14	3⅜" × 3⅝"	24" × 3⅝"
Aida 18	2⅝" × 2¾"	18⅝" × 2¾"
Hardanger 22	2⅛" × 2¼"	15¼" × 2¼"

Stitch Count: 308 × 24 **Stitch Count:** 336 × 24

MATERIALS

Completed cross-stitch on White Linen 32 (see sample information); matching thread
White embroidery floss for hemstitching

DIRECTIONS

1. Stitch with a narrow zig-zag stitch 1" from both ends of Linen piece.

2. Hemstitch above and below the design area, using embroidery floss. Count sixteen threads above and below design area. Remove the next eight threads. Working in groups of four threads, hemstitch the top edge of the upper area and the bottom edge of the lower area.

3. Slipstitch ¼" deep hem in both long edges of hand towel. Fringe between zig-zag and raw edge.

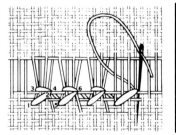

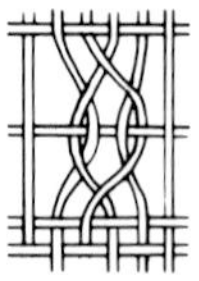

On this diagram only, one thread stands for four threads of fabric.

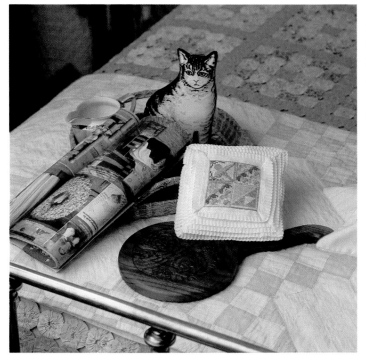

CONVERSATION PIECES

SAMPLE - Mixed Vegetable Conversation Piece

Stitched on white Belfast Linen 32 over two threads, the finished design size is 2⅞" × 2⅞". The fabric was cut 8" × 8"

FABRIC	DESIGN SIZES
Aida 11	4⅛" × 4⅛"
Aida 14	3¼" × 3¼"
Aida 18	2½" × 2½"
Hardanger 22	2⅛" × 2⅛"

Stitch Count: 46 × 46

MATERIALS

Completed cross-stitch on white Belfast Linen 32; matching thread
One 7" × 7" piece of unstitched white Belfast Linen 32
3 yards of ¾"-wide white flat trim
Stuffing
Dressmaker's pen

DIRECTIONS

All seam allowances are ¼".

1. Trim design piece 2" outside stitched border.

2. Stitch together right sides of the design piece and the unstitched piece, leaving a small opening.

3. Mark five ⅜" invervals outside each edge of the design, beginning at edge of stitching. Cut trim into the following lengths: 17½", 19½", 21½", 23½" and 25½".

4. Pin longest trim to outside marks on the design piece, folding a mitered corner and overlapping the ends. Trim excess and slipstitch to the design piece. Repeat with the remaining pieces, placing the shortest one very close to the stitching.

5. Stuff firmly. Slipstitch the opening closed.

SAMPLE - Lettuce Conversation Piece

Stitched on White Belfast Linen 32 over two threads, the finished design size is 2¾" × 2¾". The fabric was cut 8" × 8".

FABRIC	DESIGN SIZES
Aida 11	4⅛" × 4⅛"
Aida 14	3¼" × 3¼"
Aida 18	2½" × 2½
Hardanger 22	2" × 2"

Stitch Count: 45 × 45

MATERIALS

Completed cross-stitch on white Belfast Linen 32; matching thread
One 6" × 6" and one 1½" × 24½" piece of unstitched white Belfast Linen 32
2 yards of ⅛"-wide blue-green silk ribbon; matching thread
1½ yards of 1"-wide tan flat lace; matching thread
Stuffing
Dressmaker's pen

DIRECTIONS

All seam allowances are ¼".

1. Trim the design piece 2" outside stitched border.

2. Stitch the gusset strip to right sides of design piece. Join ends of the gusset.

3. Cut lace into two equal lengths. Overlap half of the width. Sew together with a running stitch. Slipstitch lace on right side of the design piece ¼" outside edge of stitching, beginning in one corner and folding ½"-deep inverted pleats in each corner.

4. Stitch the gusset and back with right sides together, leaving a small opening. Turn. Stuff. Slipstitch the opening closed.

5. Fold two or three loops of random size in ribbon. Tack to corner of design piece over ends of lace. Continue to make loops and tack to design piece, using all of the ribbon.

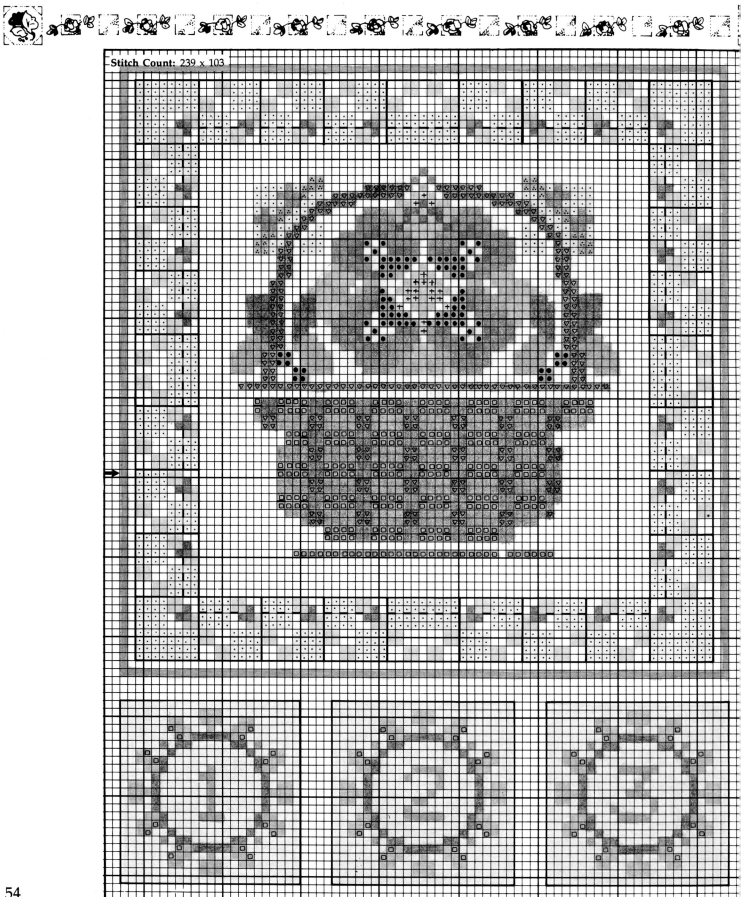

Stitch Count: 239 x 103

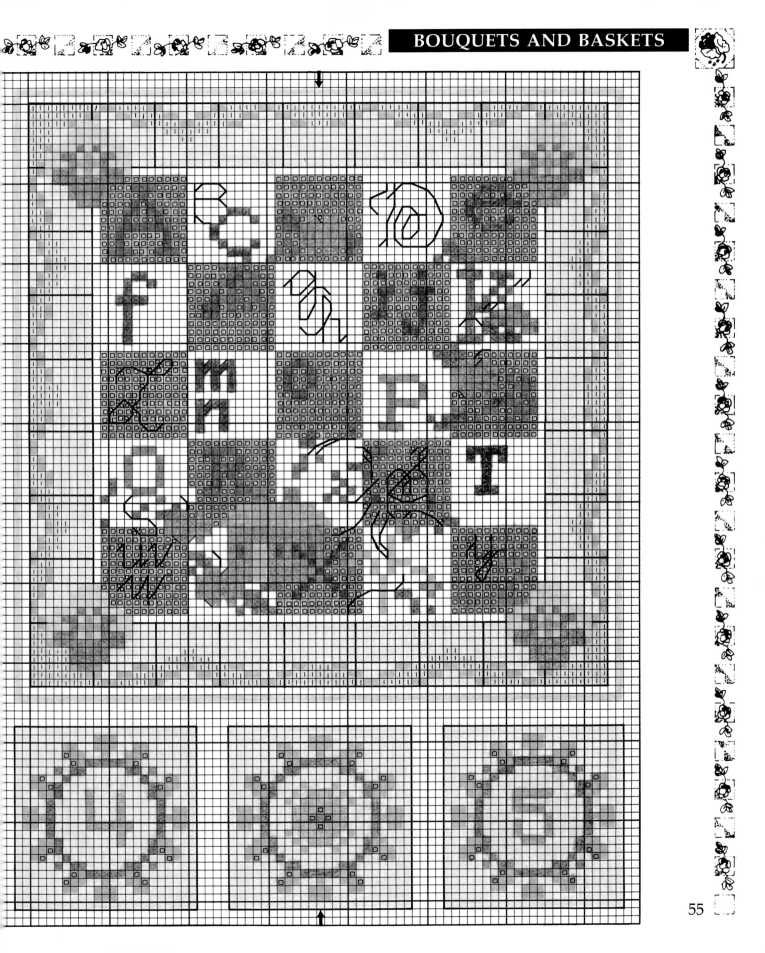

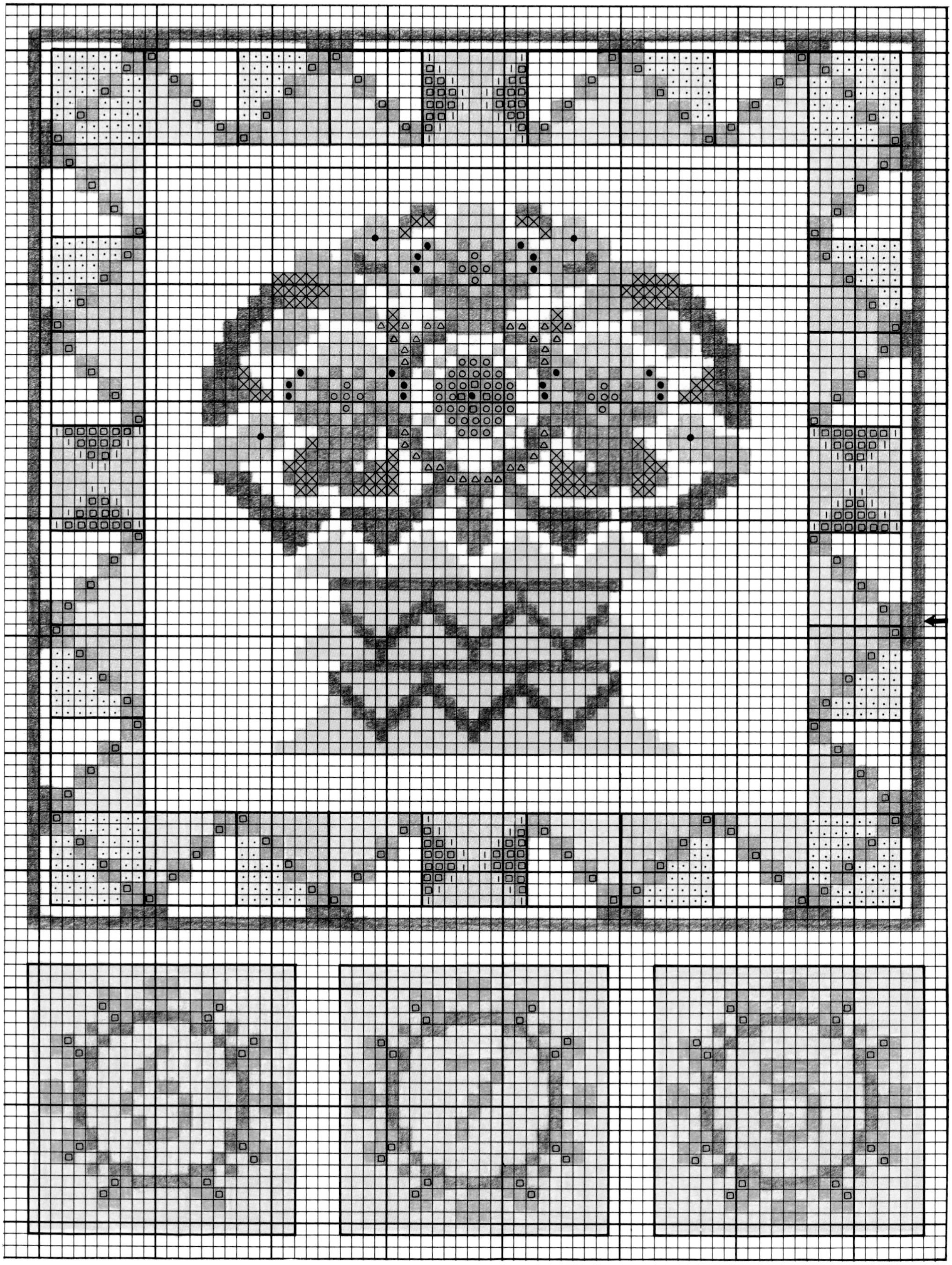

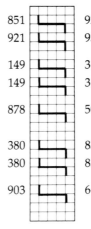

SAMPLE

Stitched on Cream Jobelan 28 over two threads, the finished design size is 17⅛″ × 7⅜″. The fabric was cut 24″ × 14″.

FABRIC	DESIGN SIZES
Aida 11	21¾″ × 9⅜″
Aida 14	17⅛″ × 7⅜″
Aida 18	13¼″ × 5¾″
Hardanger 22	10⅞″ × 4⅝″

ANCHOR		DMC (used for sample)

Step One: Cross-stitch (two strands)

4146	·	950 Sportsman Flesh-lt.
868		758 Terra Cotta-lt.
5975		356 Terra Cotta-med.
893		224 Shell Pink-lt.
894	●	223 Shell Pink-med.
42		3350 Dusty Rose-vy. dk.
869		3042 Antique Violet-lt.
101		327 Antique Violet-dk.
167		597 Turquoise
168	○	518 Wedgewood-lt.
849	◻	927 Slate Green-med.
851		924 Slate Green-vy. dk.
921		931 Antique Blue-med.
149		311 Navy Blue-med.
213	+	504 Blue Green-lt.
876	⋰	502 Blue Green
878		501 Blue Green-dk.
214		368 Pistachio Green-lt.
215	✕	320 Pistachio Green-med.
859		523 Fern Green-lt.
860	△	3052 Gray Green-med.
942		738 Tan-vy. lt.
362		437 Tan-lt.
933	ı	543 Beige Brown-utlra vy. lt.
378		841 Beige Brown-lt.
379	◓	840 Beige Brown-med.
380		839 Beige Brown-dk.
903		640 Beige Gray-vy. dk.
8581		646 Beaver Gray-dk.

Step Two: Backstitch (one strand)

851		924 Slate Green-vy. dk. (letter B)
921		931 Antique Blue-med. (left side border lines, dotted lines in basket)
149		311 Navy Blue-med. (letters L,S,U,V,W,Y)
149		311 Navy Blue-med. (two strands) (letter H)
878		501 Blue Green-dk. (dotted line in left block, middle border lines, flower stems)
380		839 Beige Brown-dk. (letter D, apple stems)
380		839 Beige Brown-dk. (two strands) (letter G)
903		640 Beige Gray-vy. dk. (right side border lines, bottom blocks)

Step Three: French knots (one strand)

878	●	501 Blue Green-dk.

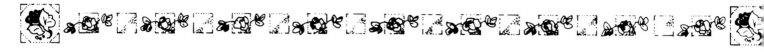

SAMPLE - TABLES FOR TEATIME

Stitched on Driftwood Belfast Linen 32 over two
threads, the finished design size is 4¾" × 4¾". The
fabric was cut 10" × 10". Complete table tops according to manufacturer's instructions.

FABRIC	DESIGN SIZES
Aida 11	7" × 7"
Aida 14	5½" × 5½"
Aida 18	4¼" × 4¼"
Hardanger 22	3½" × 3½"

Stitch Count: 77 × 77

SAMPLE - SIMPLE SACHETS

Stitched on Peach Blush, Cameo Rose or Lemon
Cream Hampton Square 30 over two threads, the finished design size is 1⅜" × 1⅜". The fabric was cut
5" × 12", allowing three whole squares. Stitch the
motif in the top square.

FABRIC	DESIGN SIZES
Aida 11	1⅞" × 1⅞"
Aida 14	1½" × 1½"
Aida 18	1⅛" × 1⅛"
Hardanger 22	1" × 1"

Stitch Count: 21 × 21

MATERIALS

Completed cross-stitch on Hampton Square 30;
   matching thread
Potpourri

DIRECTIONS

1. Cut fabric 3½" × 10½". Fold with right sides
together to measure 3½" × 5¼", matching woven
pattern in fabric.

2. Stitch sides. Fill with potpourri as desired.

Stitch Count: 103 × 120

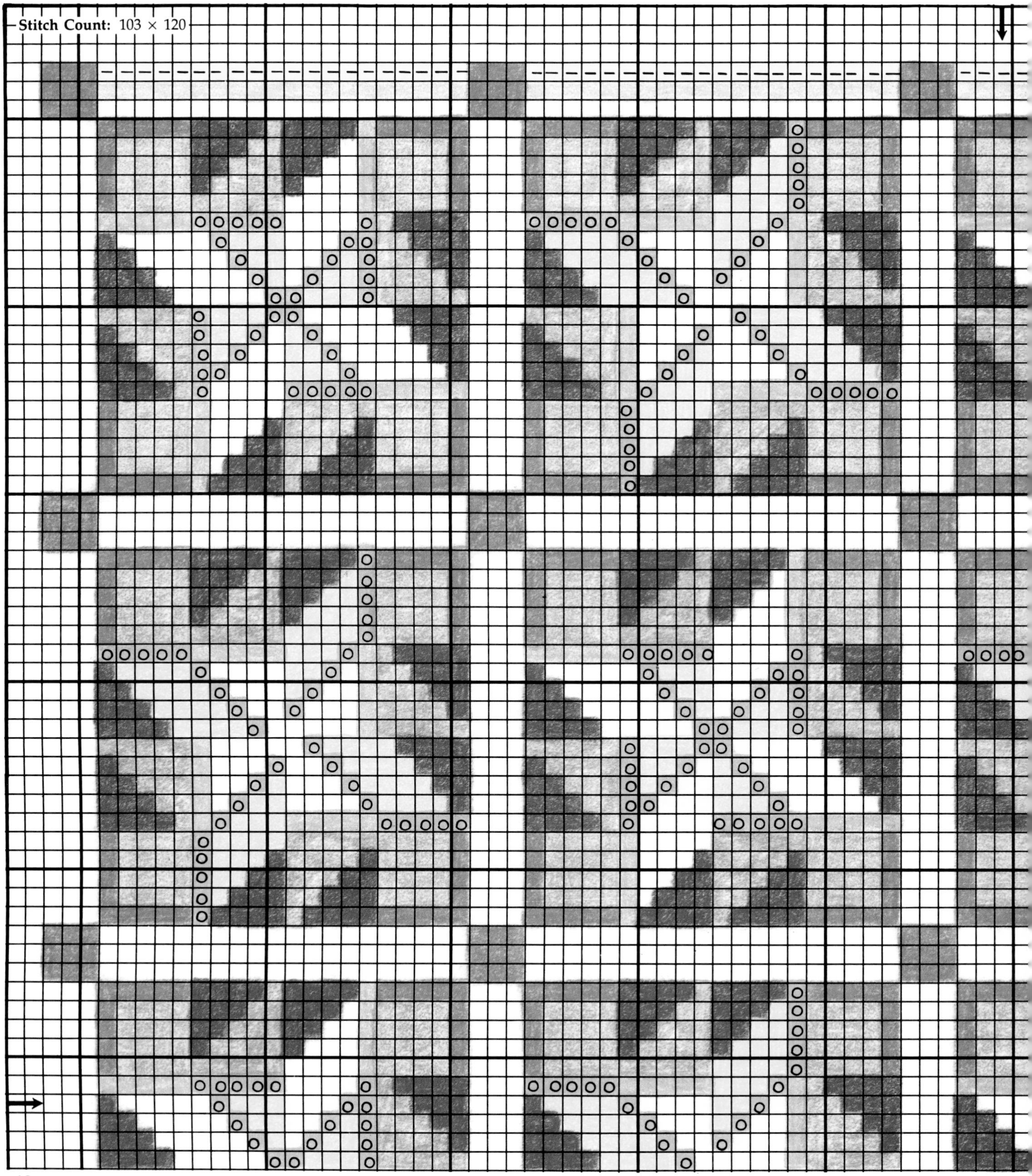

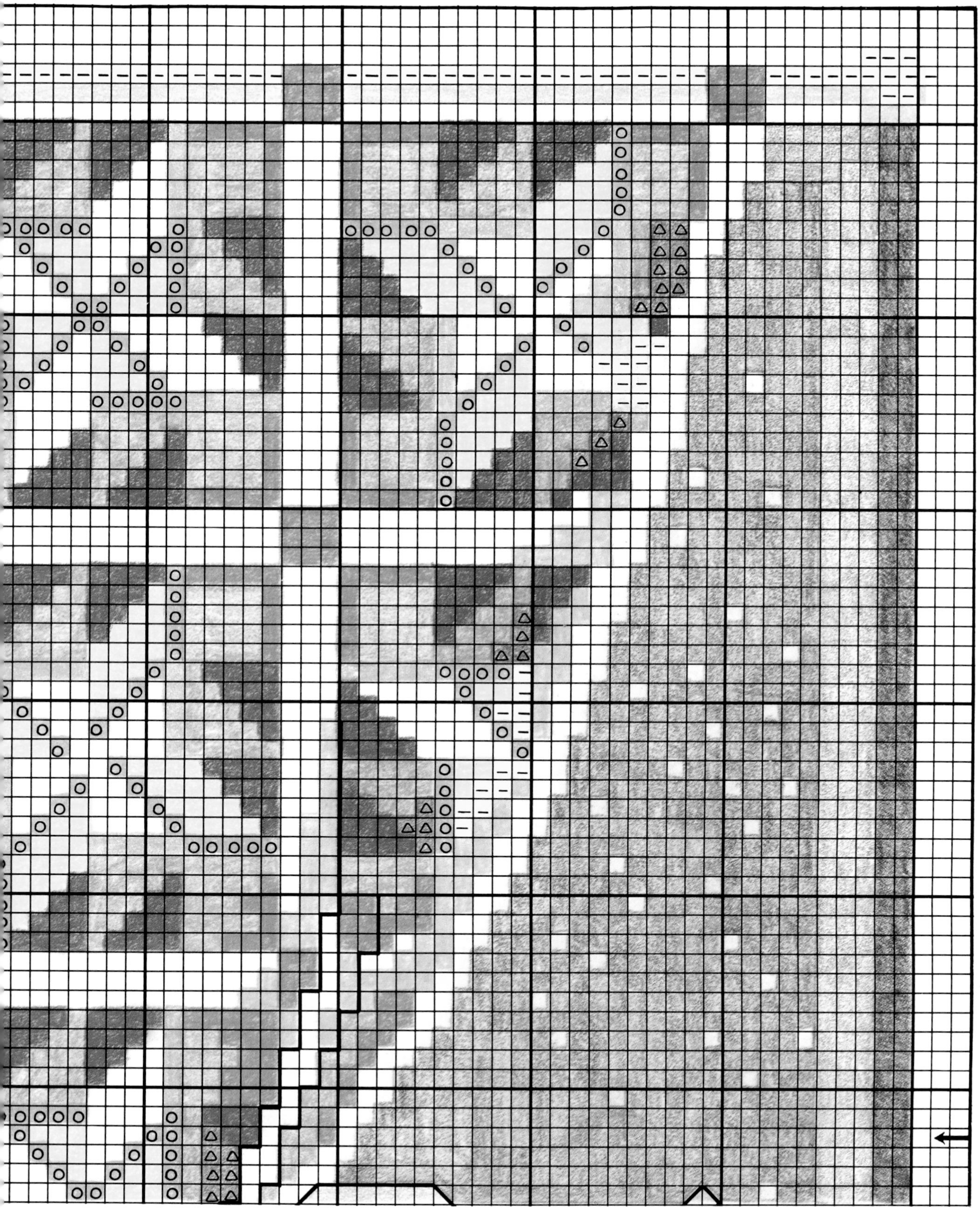

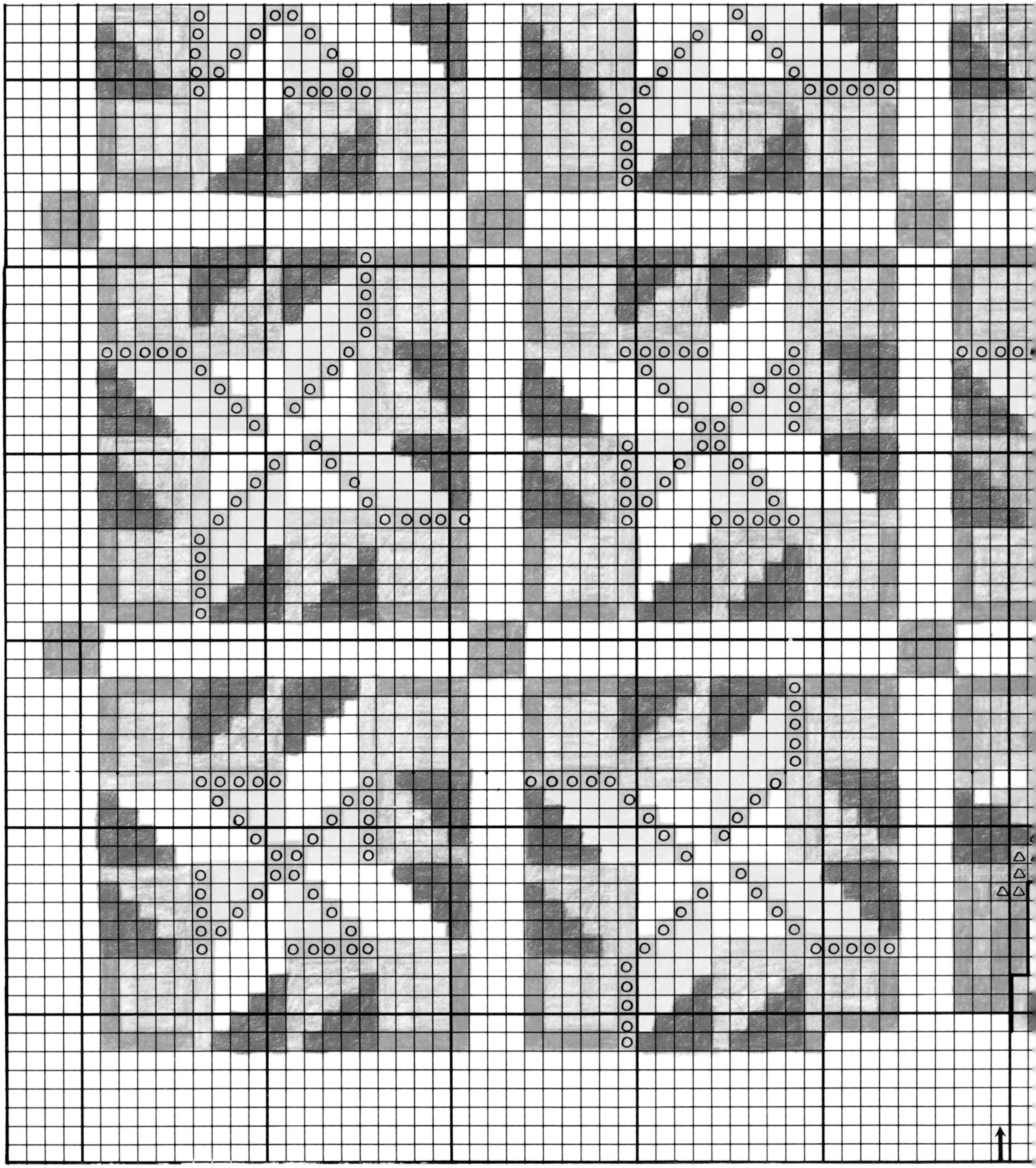

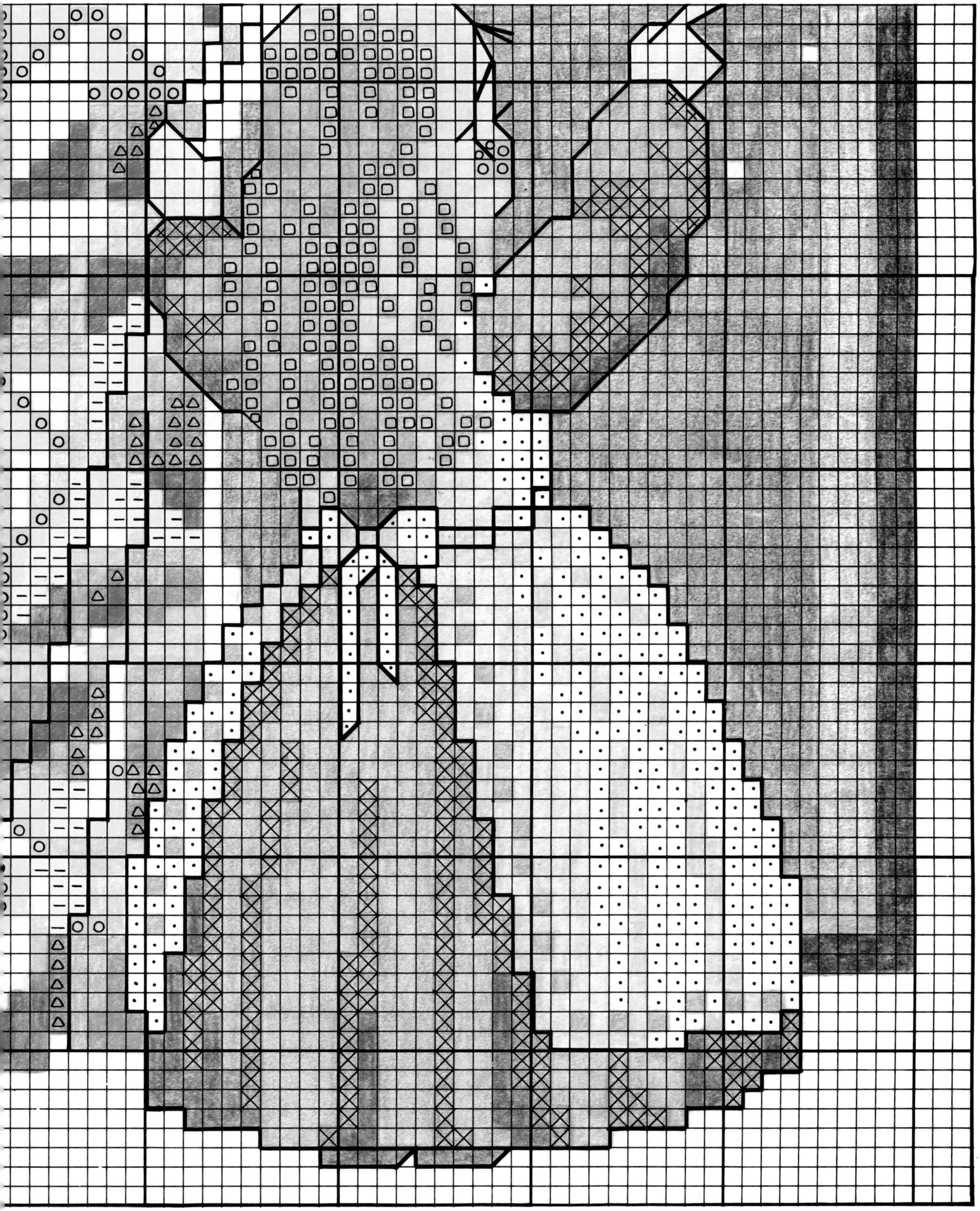

SAMPLE

Stitched on White Aida 18 over one thread, the finished design size is 5¾″ × 6⅝″. The fabric was cut 12″ × 13″.

FABRIC	DESIGN SIZES
Aida 11	9⅜″ × 10 ⅞″
Aida 14	7⅜″ × 8⅝″
Hardanger 22	4⅝″ × 5½″

ANCHOR   **DMC** (used for sample)

Step One: Cross-stitch (two strands)

1	White
300	745 Yellow-lt. pale
886	677 Old Gold-vy. lt.
891	676 Old Gold-lt.
4146	754 Peach Flesh-lt.
8	353 Peach Flesh
25	3326 Rose-lt.
66	3688 Mauve-med.
69	3687 Mauve
70	3685 Mauve-dk.
158	747 Sky Blue-vy. lt.
167	598 Turquoise-lt.
120	794 Cornflower Blue-lt.
121	793 Cornflower Blue-med.
940	792 Cornflower Blue-dk.
149	311 Navy Blue-med.
307	977 Golden Brown-lt.
308	976 Golden Brown-med.
355	975 Golden Brown-dk.
363	436 Tan
370	434 Brown-lt.
371	433 Brown-med.
397	762 Pearl Gray-vy. lt.

Step Two: Backstitch (one strand)

70	3685 Mauve-dk. (girl's dress)
121	793 Cornflower Blue-med. (curtain)
371	433 Brown-med. (hands, face, hair and shoes)

A BOX FULL OF WISHES
SIDE PATTERN
(See instructions for cutting)

66

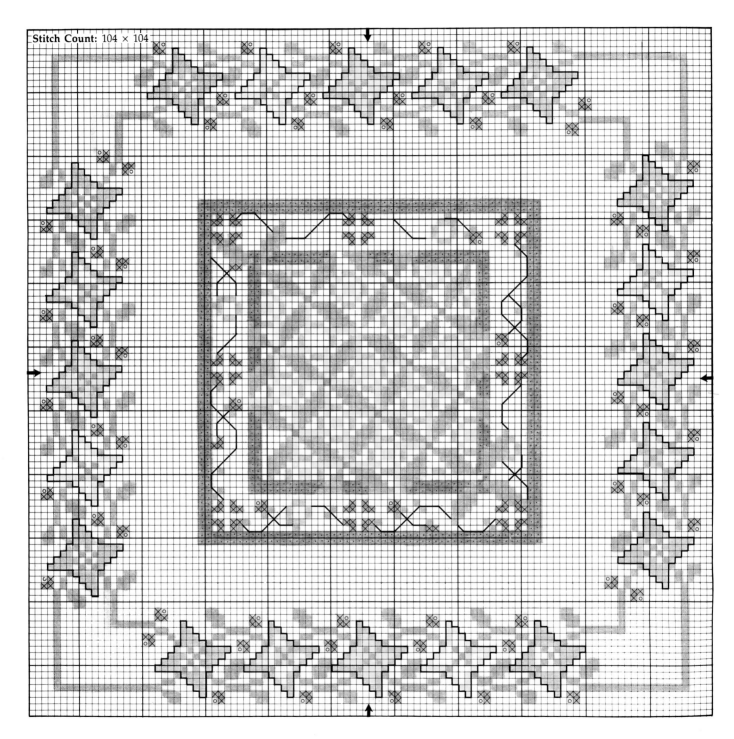

Stitch Count: 104 × 104

SAMPLE – A BOX FULL OF WISHES

Stitched on White Aida 18 over one thread, the finished design size is 5¾″ × 5¾″. The fabric was cut 10″ × 10″.

FABRIC	DESIGN SIZES
Aida 11	9½″ × 9½″
Aida 14	7⅜″ × 7⅜″
Hardanger 22	4¾″ × 4¾″

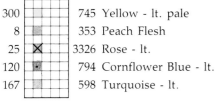

ANCHOR	DMC (used for sample)
	Step One: Cross-stitch (two strands)
300	745 Yellow - lt. pale
8	353 Peach Flesh
25	3326 Rose - lt.
120	794 Cornflower Blue - lt.
167	598 Turquoise - lt.

Step Two: Backstitch (one strand)

25	3326 Rose - lt. (star designs)
876	502 Blue Green (flower stems)

Step Three: Beads

	148T Pale Peach
	143T Robin's Egg Blue

MATERIALS

Completed cross-stitch on white Aida 18; matching thread
¼ yard unstitched white Aida 18
¼ yard white fabric for lining
Lightweight cardboard
Stuffing
One purchased rayon tassle
⅜ yard of ¼″–wide variegated apricot ribbon

DIRECTIONS

All seam allowances are ¼″.

1. Trim design piece ½″ outside border in corners.

2. Make pattern for side panel. From unstitched Aida, cut one piece to match the top piece. Also cut four side panel pieces. From lining fabric, cut four side panel pieces and two 5¾″ square pieces for bottom.

3. From cardboard, cut two 5″ squares for top and bottom and four 2½″ × 5½″ pieces for side panels.

4. Stitch one Aida side panel and one lining side panel with right sides together, leaving one end open. Clip corners. Turn. Insert cardboard and stuff moderately around all sides of cardboard. Slipstitch opening closed. Repeat for three remaining sides.

5. For top, stitch design piece and unstitched top piece with right sides together, leaving opening in one edge. Clip corners. Turn. Insert cardboard and stuff firmly. Slipstitch opening closed.

6. For bottom, stitch two lining pieces together, leaving one edge open. Clip corners. Turn. Insert cardboard and stuff firmly (one side only). Slipstitch opening closed.

7. Slipstitch side panels together at each corner, using a double strand of matching thread. Then slipstitch bottom to box with flat side to the outside. Slipstitch back of lid to top edge of one side panel.

8. Thread ribbon through tassle, center, and knot 1″ from tassle. Tie 2″-wide box next to knot. Tack to center front of lid.

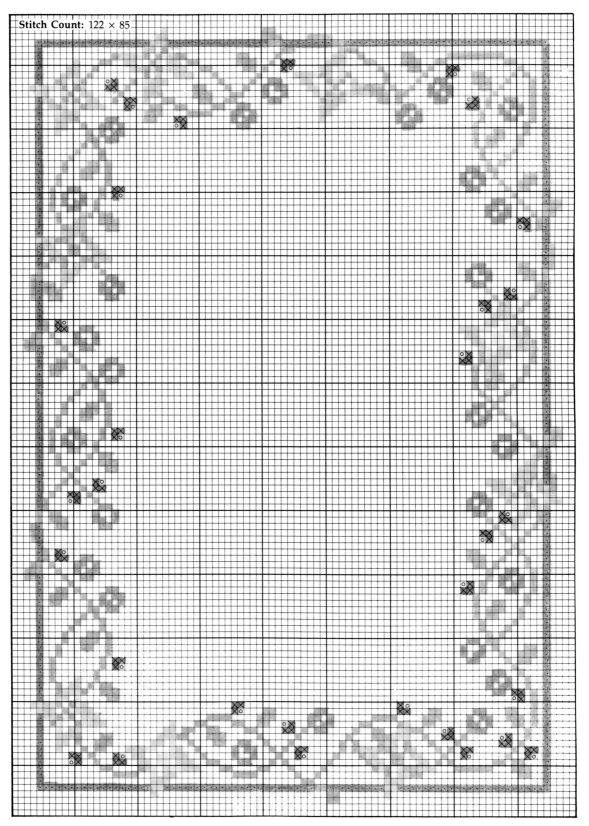

Stitch Count: 122 × 85

SAMPLE — A PICTURE-PERFECT BORDER

Stitched on White Aida 18 over one thread, the finished design size is 4¾″ × 6¾″. The fabric was cut 10″ × 12″.

FABRIC	DESIGN SIZES
Aida 11	7¾″ × 11⅛″
Aida 14	6⅛″ × 8¾″
Hardanger 22	3⅞″ × 5½″

ANCHOR   DMC (used for sample)

Step One: Cross-stitch (two strands)

300	745	Yellow - lt. pale
8	761	Salmon - lt.
25	3326	Rose - lt.
66	3688	Mauve - med.
120	794	Cornflower Blue - lt.
167	598	Turquoise - lt.

Step Two: Beads

	148T	Pale Peach

MATERIALS

Completed cross-stitch on White Aida 18
    Professionally cut mat (see Step 1)
Glue
Masking tape
Dressmakers' pen
Pencil

DIRECTIONS

1. Have a professional framer cut the mat board. The outside dimensions are 9½″ × 7½″. The window dimensions are 4¾″ × 2¾″.

2. Trim the fabric to measure 11″ × 10″ with the design centered.

3. Place the fabric wrong side up on a flat surface. Center the mat over the fabric and trace the inside edge of the mat. Also make a pen line 1″ inside the window. Cut along the inside pen line. Snip the corners between the two pen lines at a 45-degree angle.

4. Run a line of glue along the top inside edge of the mat. Fold the fabric over the mat and tape at two or three points, making sure that the inside stitching line is parallel to the inside edge of the mat.

5. Repeat Step 4 for the bottom inside edge; then the sides.

6. Run a line of glue along the top outside edge of the mat to within 2″ of the corners. Fold the fabric over the edge, pulling the surface taut. Tape. Repeat along the bottom edge; then the sides. Trim the excess fabric from the corners on the back. Drop the mat into a ready-made frame or have a professional framer complete the framing.

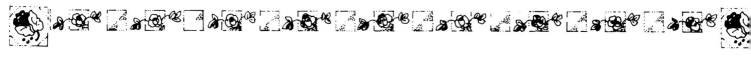

Stitch Count: 139 × 195

SAMPLE

Stitched on Cream Belfast Linen 32 over two threads, the finished design size is 8¾″ × 12¼″. The fabric was cut 15″ × 18″.

FABRIC	DESIGN SIZES
Aida 11	12⅝″ × 17¾″
Aida 14	9⅞″ × 13⅞″
Aida 18	7¾″ × 10⅞″
Hardanger 22	6⅜″ × 8⅞″

ANCHOR   **DMC** (used for sample)

Step One: Cross-stitch (two strands)

ANCHOR		DMC	
4146		754	Peach Flesh-lt.
8	o	761	Salmon-lt.
25		3326	Rose-lt.
66		3688	Mauve-med.
119		333	Blue Violet-dk.
128		800	Delft-pale
130	X	799	Delft-med.
131		798	Delft-dk.
213		369	Pistachio Green-vy. lt.
214	△	368	Pistachio Green-lt.
215		320	Pistachio Green-med.
246		319	Pistachio Green-vy. dk.
885	·	739	Tan-ultra vy. lt.
942		738	Tan-vy. lt.
882		407	Sportsman Flesh-dk.

Step Two: Backstitch (one strand)

ANCHOR		DMC	
214		368	Pistachio Green-lt. (basket border, stems)
246		319	Pistachio Green-vy. dk. (vines)
882		407	Sportsman Flesh-dk. (top & bottom of baskets on border)

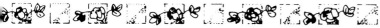

SAMPLE - RIBBON AND VOILE SACHETS

The design is taken from the center of **The Quilter's Prize**, page 73. Stitched on Cream Belfast Linen over two threads, the finished design size is 1¼″ × 1¼″. The fabric was cut 8″ × 8″. The stitch count is 21 × 21.

FABRIC	DESIGN SIZES
Aida 11	1⅞″ × 1⅞″
Aida 14	1½″ × 1½″
Aida 18	1⅛″ × 1⅛″
Hardanger 22	1″ × 1″

MATERIALS

Completed cross-stitch on cream Belfast Linen 32; matching thread
One 7″ × 7″ and one 1¼″ × 18″ piece of cream Belfast Linen 32 or matching fabric
¼ yard of cream Voile
1¼ yards of ⅜″–wide cream or apricot satin ribbon
Stuffing
Potpourri

DIRECTIONS

All seam allowances are ¼″.

1. Trace a pattern for the heart. Center over the design and cut one heart. Also cut one heart from the 7″ × 7″ piece of cream fabric.

2. Cut two hearts and one 1¼″ × 36″ gusset from the voile. Stitch gathering threads in both long edges of the voile gusset. Gather voile to fit over 1¼″ × 18″ gusset. Pin the gusset pieces together, dispersing fullness of voile evenly.

3. Pin the voile hearts over the fabric hearts. Stitch the right sides of gusset and design piece together, beginning and ending on one side of heart. Join ends of the gusset.

4. To attach ribbon, begin by placing the end at the top of the heart. Fold into 1″–wide figure-eights (see diagram). Place the center of figure-eight ⅜″ from seam. Tack figure-eights to the design piece.

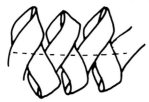

5. Pin back to gusset. Stitch, leaving a small opening. Clip the curved seam allowance. Turn. Stuff moderately, adding potpourri as desired. Slipstitch the opening closed.

SAMPLE - TOPS IN CRYSTAL

The design is taken from the center of the **Quilter's Prize**, page 73. Stitched on Cream Belfast Linen 32, the small ornament is over one thread, and the large ornament is over two threads. The small finished design size is 1″ × 1″ and the large finished design size is 2″ × 2″. The fabric was cut 5″ × 5″. The stitch count is 33 × 33. Insert in jar lid following manufacturer's instructions.

FABRIC	DESIGN SIZES
Aida 11	3″ × 3″
Aida 14	2⅜″ × 2⅜″
Aida 18	1⅞″ × 1⅞″
Hardanger 22	1½″ × 1½″

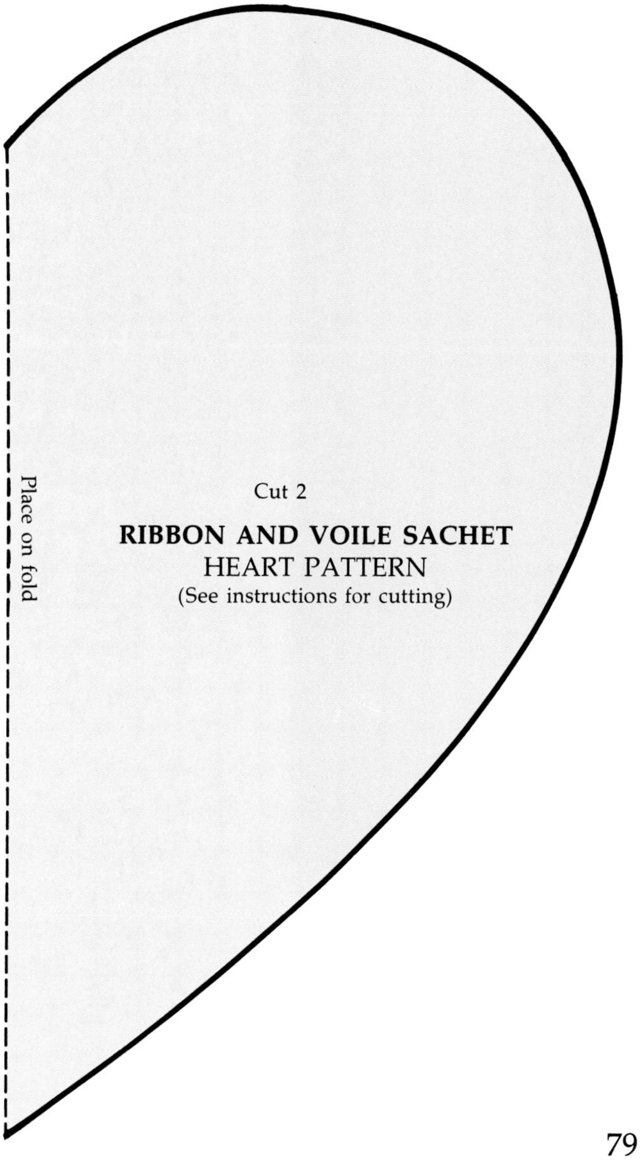

Place on fold

Cut 2

RIBBON AND VOILE SACHET
HEART PATTERN
(See instructions for cutting)

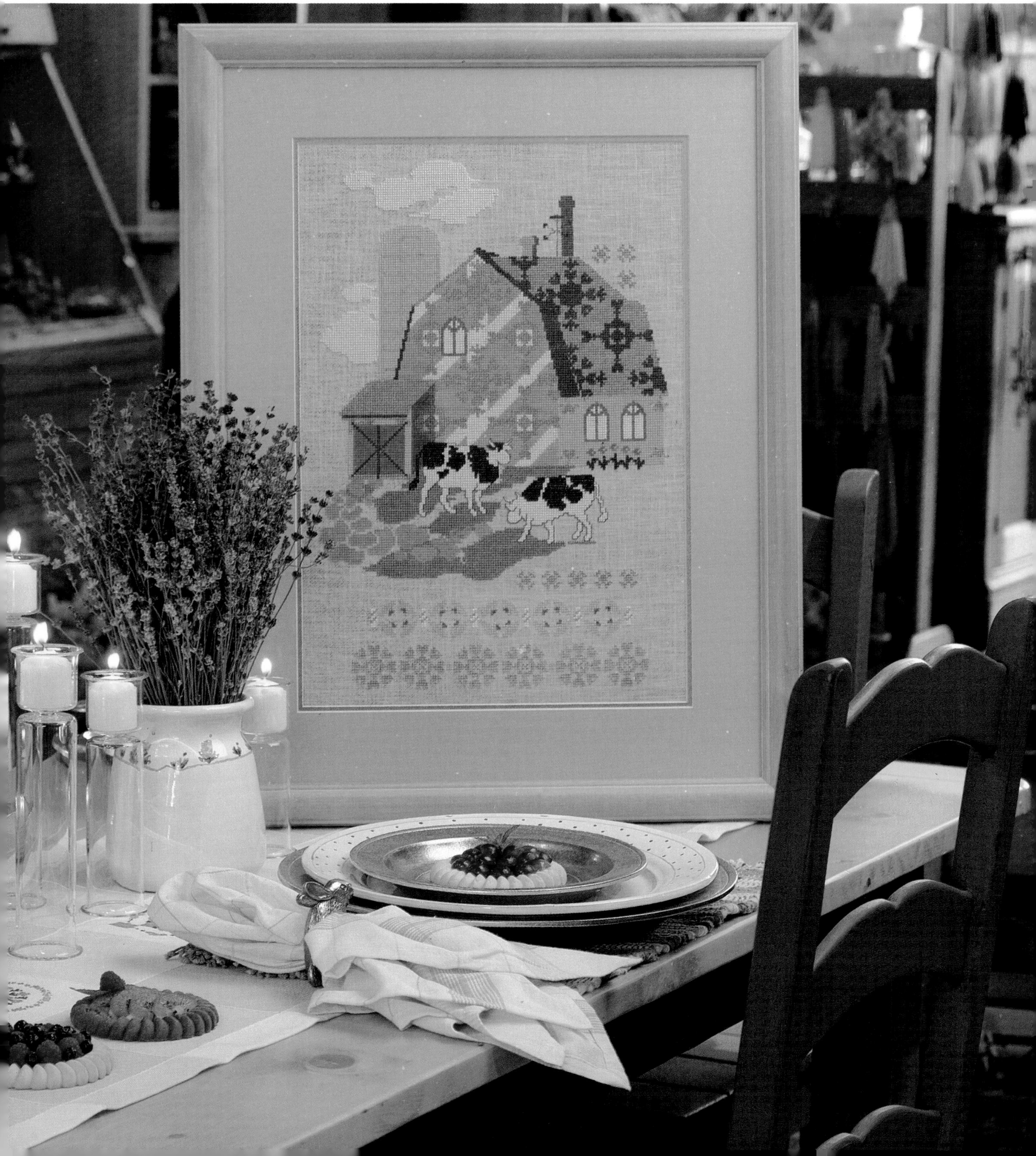

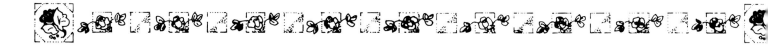

Stitch Count: 150 × 224

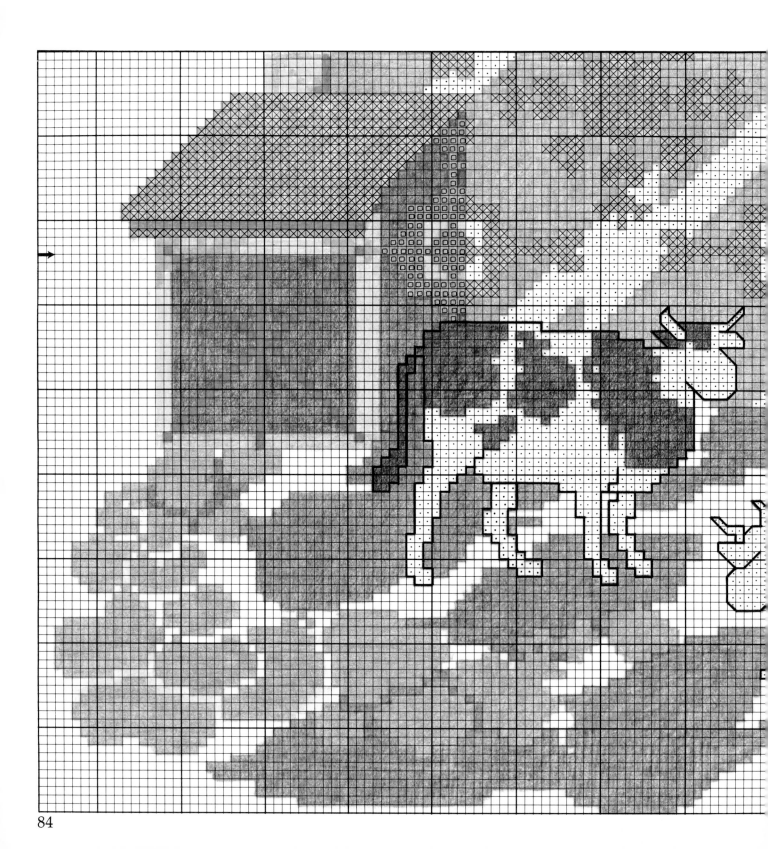

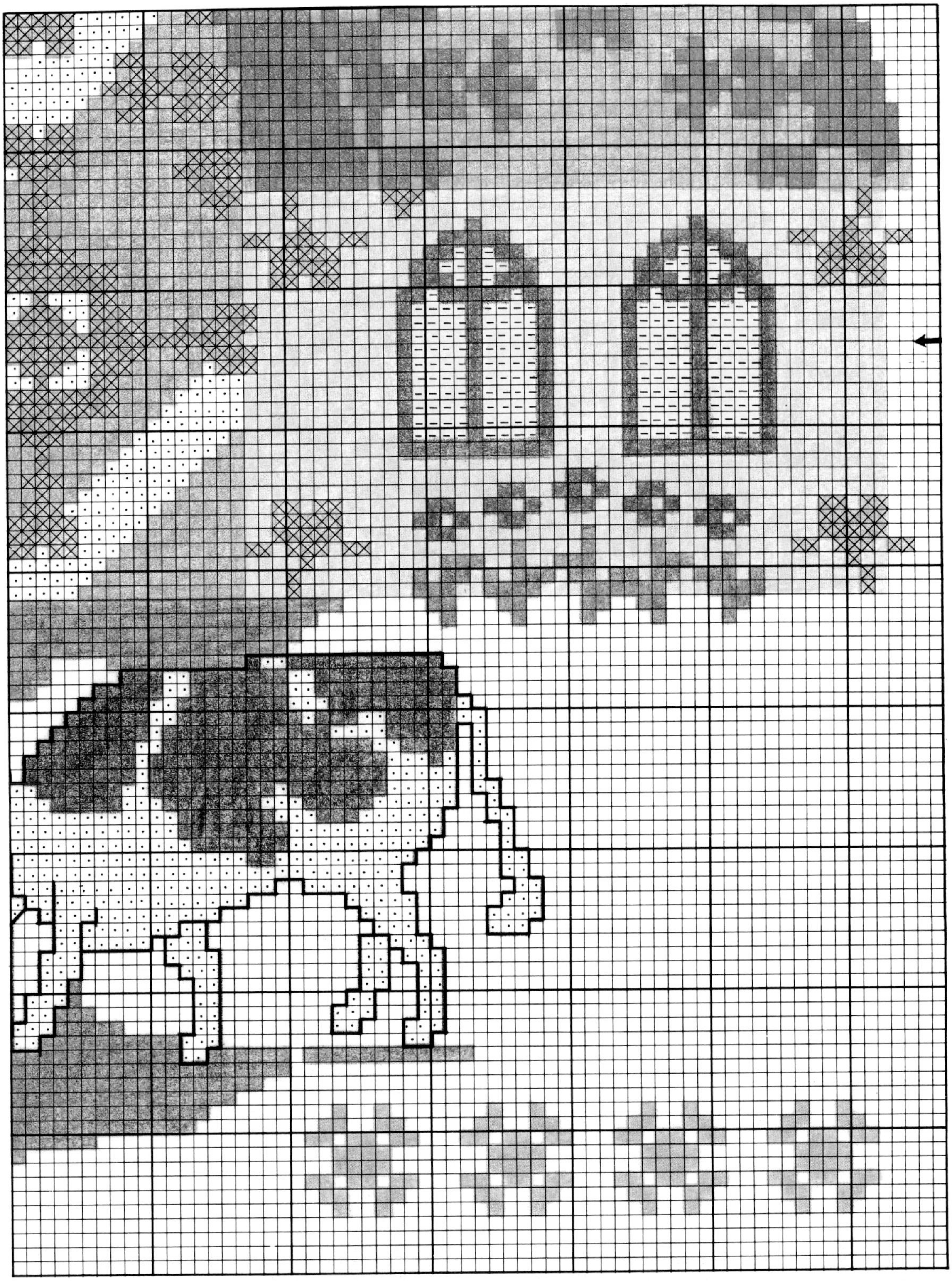

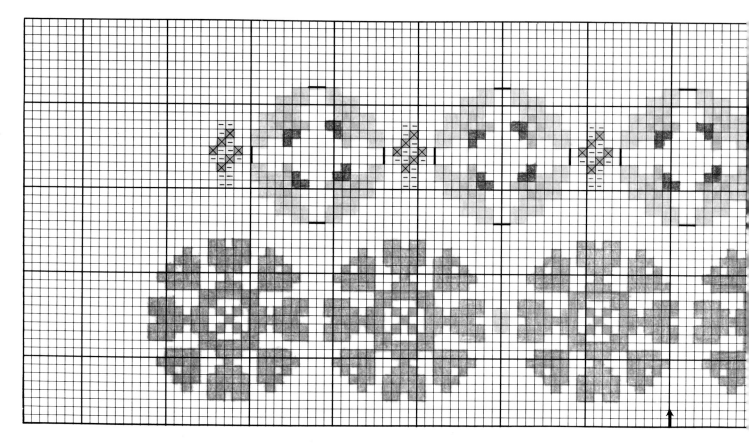

SAMPLE

Stiched on Sand Dublin 25 over two threads, the finished design size is 12″ × 17 ⅞″. The fabric was cut 19″ × 24″.

FABRIC	DESIGN SIZES
Aida 11	13¾″ × 20⅜″
Aida 14	10¾″ × 16″
Aida 18	8⅜″ × 12½″
Hardanger 22	6⅞″ × 10⅛″

ANCHOR **DMC** (used for sample)

Step One: Cross-stitch (two strands)

		926 Ecru
300		745 Yellow-lt. pale
868		758 Terra Cotta-lt.
882		407 Sportsman Flesh-dk.
869		3042 Antique Violet-lt.
871		3041 Antique Violet-med.

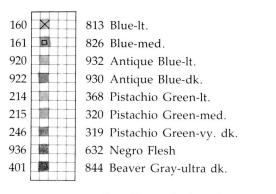

160	☒	813 Blue-lt.
161	▫	826 Blue-med.
920		932 Antique Blue-lt.
922		930 Antique Blue-dk.
214		368 Pistachio Green-lt.
215		320 Pistachio Green-med.
246		319 Pistachio Green-vy. dk.
936		632 Negro Flesh
401		844 Beaver Gray-ultra dk.

Step Two: Backstitch (one strand)

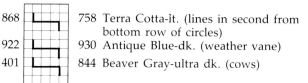

868		758 Terra Cotta-lt. (lines in second from bottom row of circles)
922		930 Antique Blue-dk. (weather vane)
401		844 Beaver Gray-ultra dk. (cows)

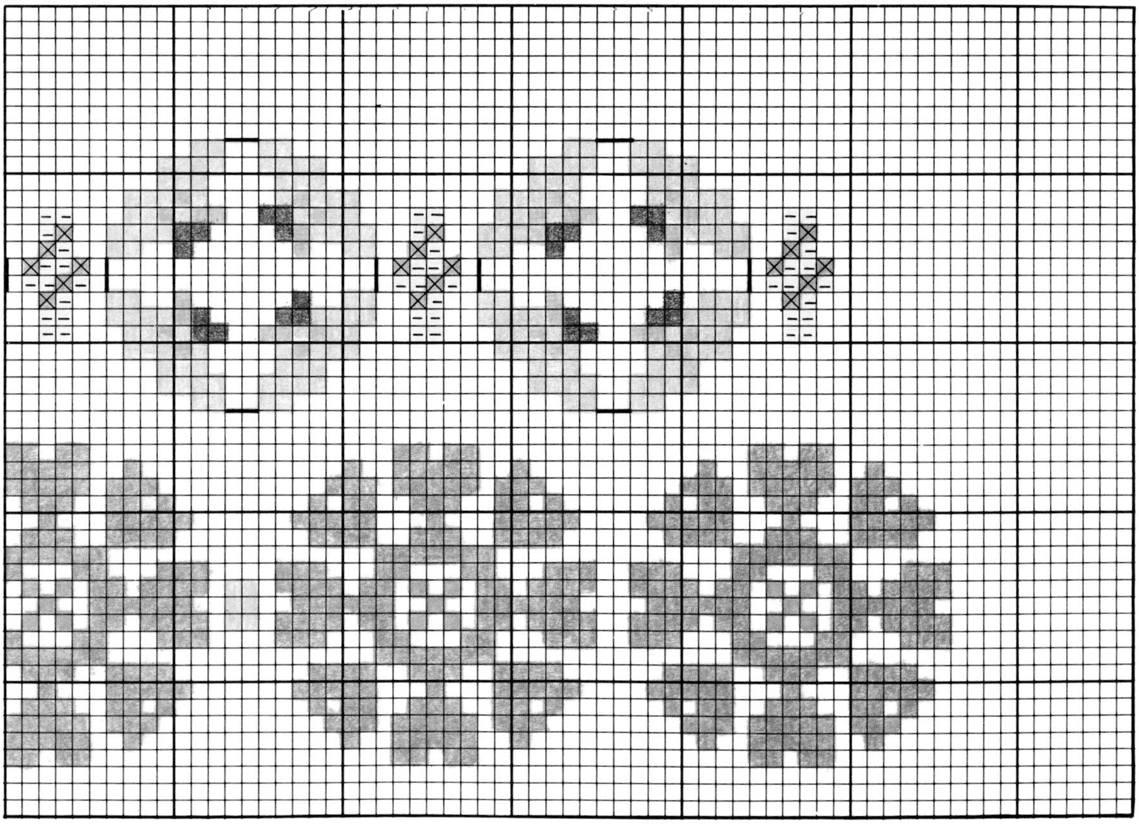

SQUARE

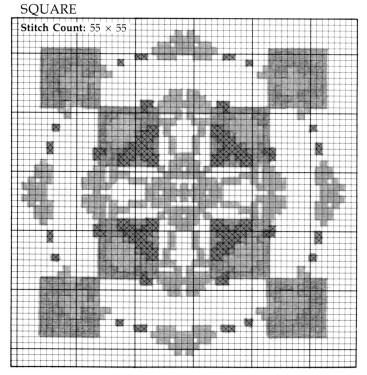

Stitch Count: 55 × 55

ROUND

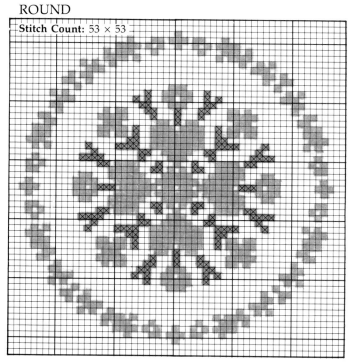

Stitch Count: 53 × 53

DIAMOND

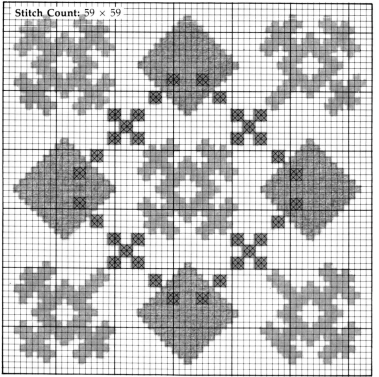

Stitch Count: 59 × 59

SAMPLE – A TABLE RUNNER

The table runner was stitched on Green/White Alice 27 over two threads. The fabric was cut 21″ × 54″ to include five white squares. Center each design in the white squares with the square pattern in the middle, the round pattern on either side and the diamond pattern in the end squares. The finished design size for each pattern is: diamond–4⅜″ × 4⅜″; round–3⅞″ × 3⅞″; square–4⅛″ x 4⅛″. Trim the fabric 7½″ wider than the white squares on both sides and 2½″ longer on both ends. Zig-zag edges. Fold under 1¼″ on all edges and slipstitch.

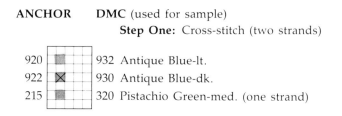

ANCHOR		DMC (used for sample)
		Step One: Cross-stitch (two strands)
920		932 Antique Blue-lt.
922		930 Antique Blue-dk.
215		320 Pistachio Green-med. (one strand)

88

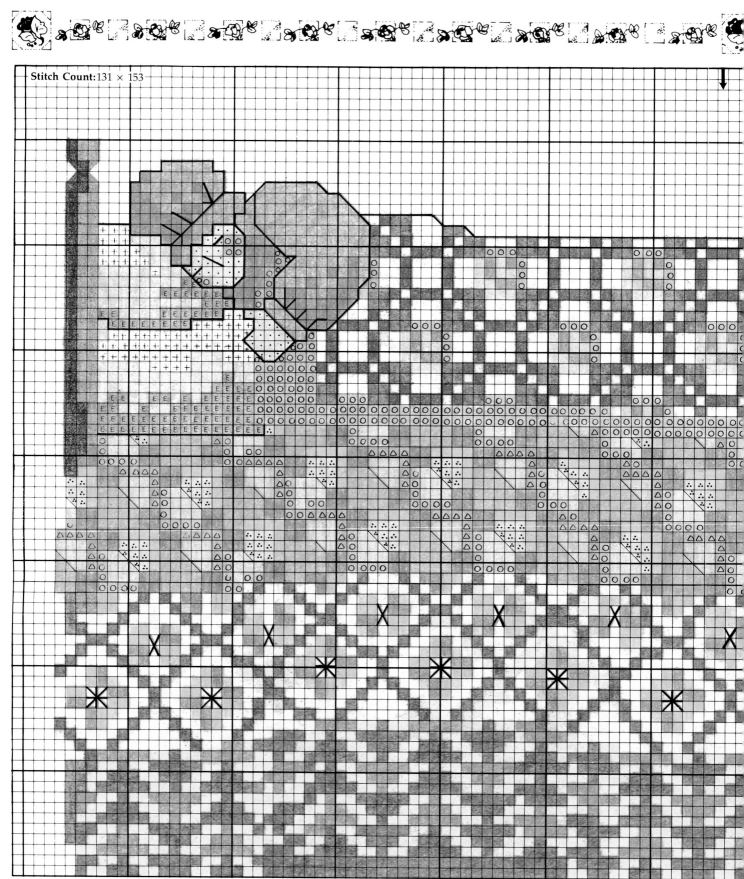

Stitch Count: 131 × 153

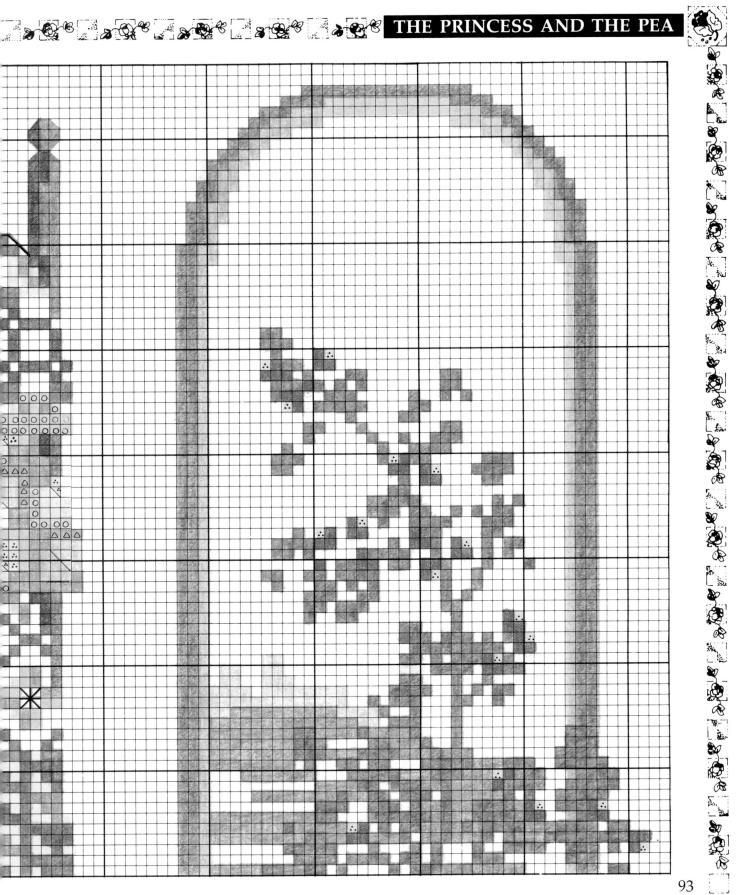

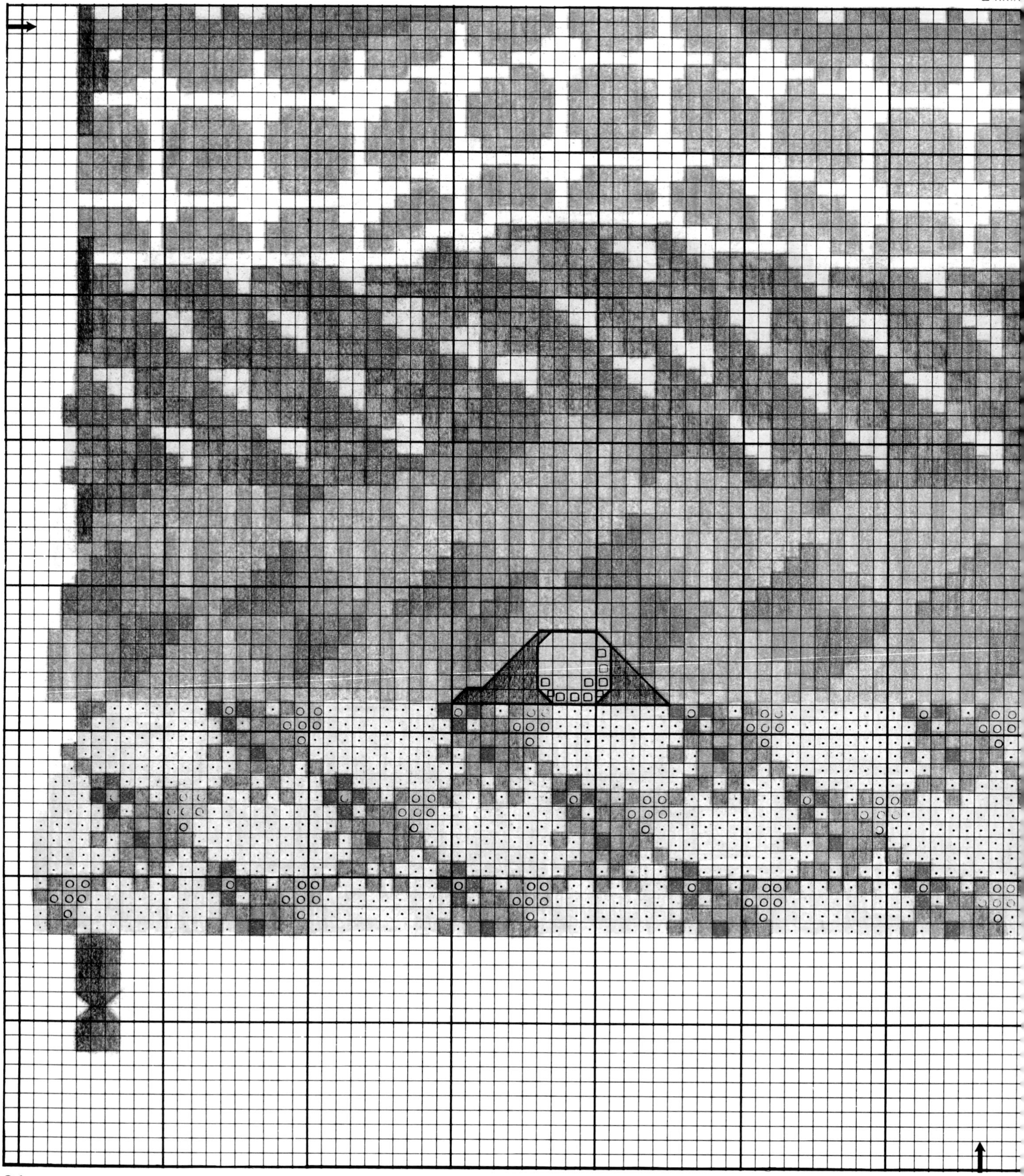

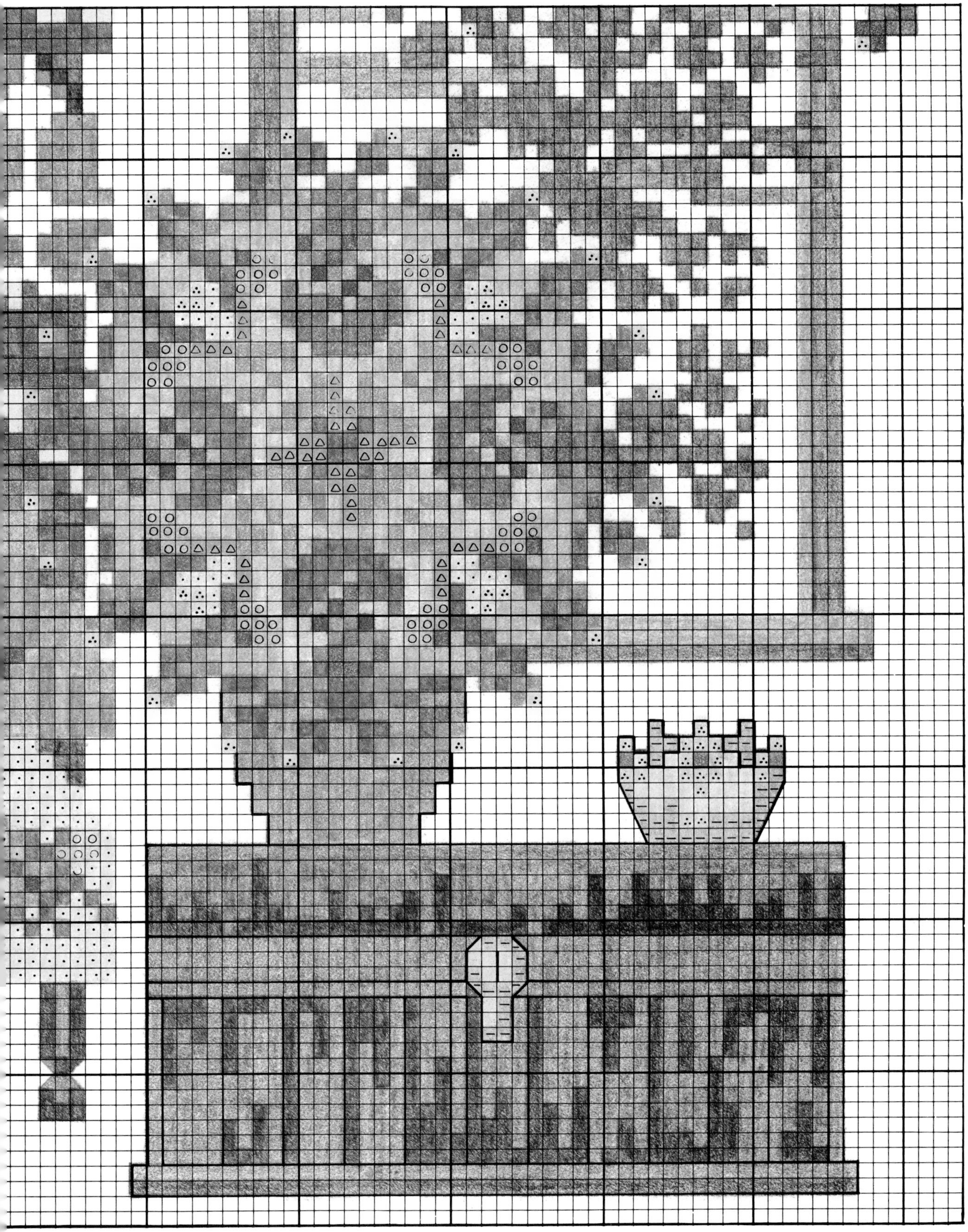

SAMPLE

Stitched on White Jobelan 28 over two threads, the finished design size is 9⅜" × 10⅞". The fabric was cut 16" × 17".

FABRIC	DESIGN SIZES
Aida 11	11⅞" × 13⅞"
Aida 14	9⅜" × 10⅞"
Aida 18	7¼" × 8½"
Hardanger 22	6" × 7"

ANCHOR **DMC** (used for sample)

Step One: Cross-stitch (two strands)

1	White
300	745 Yellow-lt. pale
297	743 Yellow-med.
303	742 Tangerine-lt.
306	725 Topaz
890	729 Old Gold-med.
48	818 Baby Pink
50	605 Cranberry-vy. lt.
75	604 Cranberry-lt.
76	603 Cranberry
42	3350 Dusty Rose-vy. dk.
95	554 Violet-lt.
98	553 Violet-med.
119	333 Blue Violet-dk.
128	800 Delft-pale
130	799 Delft-med.
131	798 Delft-dk.
185	964 Seagreen-lt.
186	959 Seagreen-med.
256	704 Chartreuse-bright
239	702 Kelly Green
843	3364 Pine Green (one strand)
876	502 Blue Green
203	954 Nile Green
204	912 Emerald Green-lt.
210	562 Jade-med.
212	561 Jade-vy. dk.
362	437 Tan-lt.
309	435 Brown-vy. lt.
371	433 Brown-med.

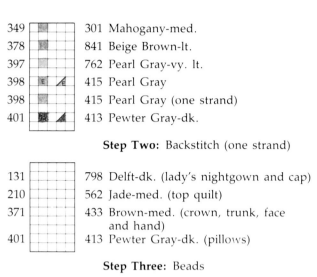

349	301 Mahogany-med.
378	841 Beige Brown-lt.
397	762 Pearl Gray-vy. lt.
398	415 Pearl Gray
398	415 Pearl Gray (one strand)
401	413 Pewter Gray-dk.

Step Two: Backstitch (one strand)

131	798 Delft-dk. (lady's nightgown and cap)
210	562 Jade-med. (top quilt)
371	433 Brown-med. (crown, trunk, face and hand)
401	413 Pewter Gray-dk. (pillows)

Step Three: Beads

	968K Red

Step Four: Smyrna Cross (one strand)

210		562 Jade-med.

SAMPLE - Twin Sheet

Stitched with Waste Canvas 14 over one thread on a white twin sheet, the finished design size is 68⅝" × 1¾". The canvas was cut in three 24" × 6" pieces. The finished design size for one motif was 1⅜" × 1¾". The motif was repeated 48 times. For a larger sheet, continue motif to edge.

SAMPLE - Pillowcase

Stitched with Waste Canvas 14 over one thread on a white standard pillow case, the complete finished design size is 22⅞" × 1¾". The canvas was cut 26" × 6". The finished design size for one motif is 1⅜" × 1¾". The motif was repeated 16 times. Remove hem from pillowcase and baste Waste Canvas to fabric. Begin stitching 1¼" from fold of hem.

SAMPLE - PINK PORCELAIN JAR

The bouquet is taken from the **Princess and the Pea**, page 95. Stitched on White Jobelan 28 over two threads, the finished design size is 3" × 3". The fabric was cut 6" × 6". The stitch count is 42 × 42. Insert in jar lid following manufacturer's instructions.

BEDDING FIT FOR A PRINCESS

MATERIALS for one twin sheet

Completed cross-stitch on one twin white top sheet; see sample information

1⅞ yards of 1″–wide flat white eyelet trim; matching thread

1⅞ yards of 3″–wide flat white eyelet trim

1⅞ yards of 2″–wide gathered white eyelet

3¾ yards of ¹/₁₆″–wide pink rayon braid*; matching thread

1⅞ yards of ⅜″–wide white satin ribbon

1⅞ yards of ⅜″–wide pink picot-edge satin ribbon

DIRECTIONS

1. Mark centers of all lengths of eyelet trim and ribbon. Cut rayon braid in half and mark centers of each length. Also mark center of hemmed edge of sheet.

2. Pin 3″–wide eyelet to hemmed edge of sheet, matching centers. Pin 2″–wide and 1″–wide eyelet trims to sheet over 3″–wide trim. Stitch all to sheet. Fold under each end of trim and hem.

3. Pin white ribbon with top edge ¾″ from edge of sheet, matching centers. Stitch to sheet. Pin pink ribbon over lower edge of white ribbon and covering all raw edges of eyelet trim. Stitch to sheet.

4. Pin pink braid ¼″ above white ribbon and ¼″ above design area. Stitch to sheet.

* The braid is easy to attach using invisible thread and a zig-zag stitch that is ¹/₁₆″–wide.

MATERIALS for one pillowcase

Completed cross-stitch design on standard white pillowcase; see sample information

1¼ yards of 1″–wide flat white eyelet trim; matching thread

1¼ yards of 3″–wide flat white eyelet trim

1¼ yards of 2″–wide gathered white eyelet

2½ yards of ¹/₁₆″–wide pink rayon braid*; matching thread

1¼ yards of ⅜″–wide white satin ribbon

1¼ yards of ⅜″–wide pink picot-edge satin ribbon

DIRECTIONS

1. Repeat Steps 1 and 2 of sheet instructions. Sew ends of each trim together. Trim excess.

2. Repeat Steps 3 and 4 of sheet instructions.

For instructions on using Waste Canvas, see page 133.

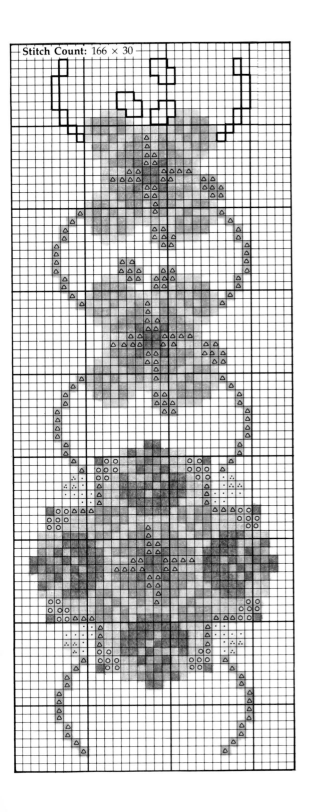

Stitch Count: 166 × 30

SAMPLE - HER ROYAL BELL PULL

Stitched on White Jobelan 28 over two threads, the finished design size is 11⅞″ × 2⅛″. The fabric was cut 7″ × 20″.

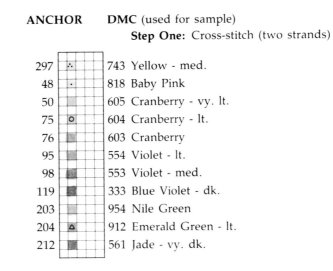

ANCHOR		DMC (used for sample)
		Step One: Cross-stitch (two strands)
297	∴	743 Yellow - med.
48	·	818 Baby Pink
50		605 Cranberry - vy. lt.
75	o	604 Cranberry - lt.
76		603 Cranberry
95		554 Violet - lt.
98		553 Violet - med.
119		333 Blue Violet - dk.
203		954 Nile Green
204	△	912 Emerald Green - lt.
212		561 Jade - vy. dk.

MATERIALS

Completed cross-stitch on white Jobelan; matching thread
Bell pull hardware for 2¼″–wide bell pull
Dressmaker's pen

DIRECTIONS

All seam allowances are ¼″.

1. Cut design piece 4¾″ × 15¼″ with design centered. Fold with right sides together to measure 2⅜″–wide. Stitch long edge. Turn. Refold with design centered on front and seam pressed open down center back.

2. Mark front of bell pull ½″ and ¾″ above and below end of design. Then fold edges to inside to make a point beyond each ¾″ mark. Thread ends through hardware to back, folding on line ½″ from design. Slipstitch point to bell pull back.

Stitch Count: 190 × 150

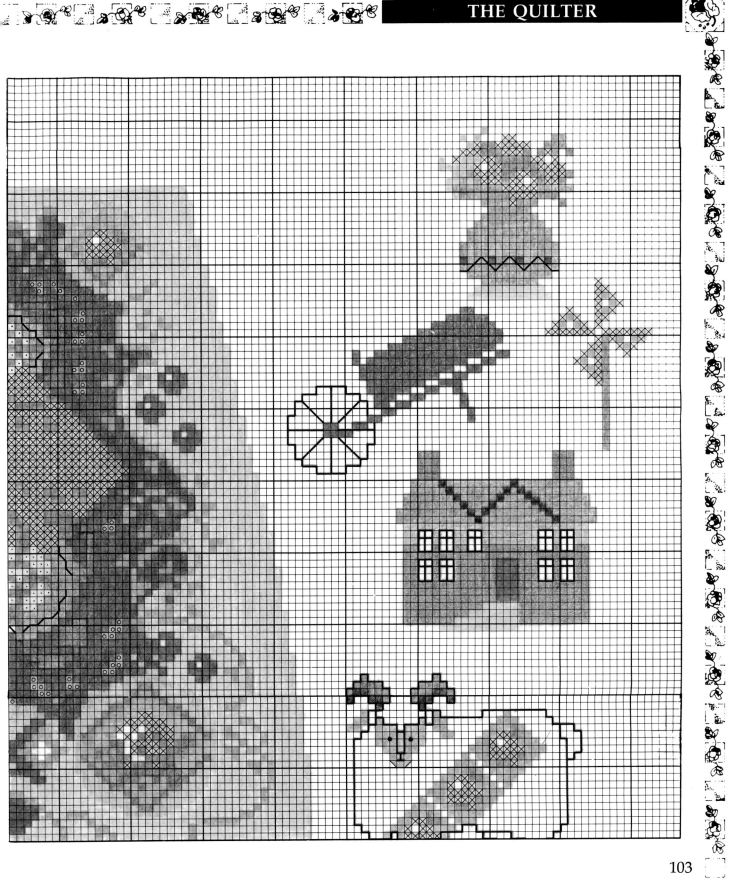

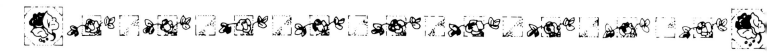

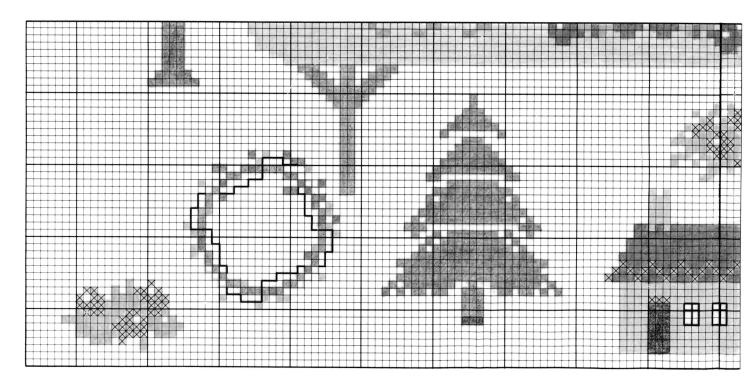

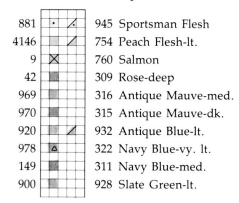

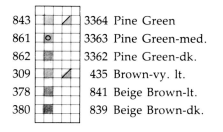

SAMPLE

Stitched on Glenshee Egyptian Quality E 18, the finished design size is 10½″ × 8⅜″. The fabric was cut 17″ × 15″.

FABRIC **DESIGN SIZES**
Aida 11   17¼″ × 13¾″
Aida 14   13⅝″ × 10¾″
Aida 18   10½″ × 8⅜″
Hardanger 22   8⅝″ × 6⅞″

ANCHOR **DMC** (used for sample)
Step One: Cross-stitch (two strands)

881	· /	945	Sportsman Flesh
4146	/	754	Peach Flesh-lt.
9	X	760	Salmon
42		309	Rose-deep
969		316	Antique Mauve-med.
970		315	Antique Mauve-dk.
920	/	932	Antique Blue-lt.
978	△	322	Navy Blue-vy. lt.
149		311	Navy Blue-med.
900		928	Slate Green-lt.

843	/	3364	Pine Green
861	o	3363	Pine Green-med.
862		3362	Pine Green-dk.
309	/	435	Brown-vy. lt.
378		841	Beige Brown-lt.
380		839	Beige Brown-dk.

Step Two: Backstitch (one strand)

970		315	Antique Mauve-dk. (windows on peach house)
149		311	Navy Blue-med. (pattern in quilt, sheep, wheel, and windows in dk. pink house)
843		3364	Pine Green (flower stems in vase)
862		3362	Pine Green-dk. (pattern in wreath)
380		839	Beige Brown-dk. (face, hand and sheep's horns)

Step Three: French knots (one strand)

149	●	311	Navy Blue-med.

104

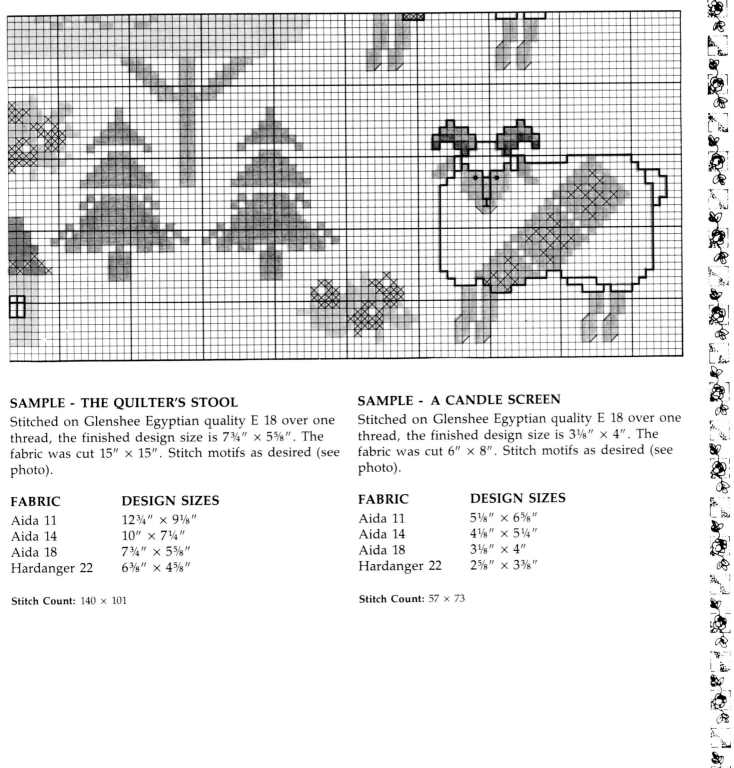

SAMPLE - THE QUILTER'S STOOL

Stitched on Glenshee Egyptian quality E 18 over one thread, the finished design size is 7¾″ × 5⅝″. The fabric was cut 15″ × 15″. Stitch motifs as desired (see photo).

FABRIC	DESIGN SIZES
Aida 11	12¾″ × 9⅛″
Aida 14	10″ × 7¼″
Aida 18	7¾″ × 5⅝″
Hardanger 22	6⅜″ × 4⅝″

Stitch Count: 140 × 101

SAMPLE - A CANDLE SCREEN

Stitched on Glenshee Egyptian quality E 18 over one thread, the finished design size is 3⅛″ × 4″. The fabric was cut 6″ × 8″. Stitch motifs as desired (see photo).

FABRIC	DESIGN SIZES
Aida 11	5⅛″ × 6⅝″
Aida 14	4⅛″ × 5¼″
Aida 18	3⅛″ × 4″
Hardanger 22	2⅝″ × 3⅜″

Stitch Count: 57 × 73

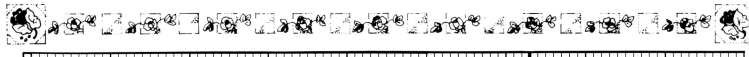

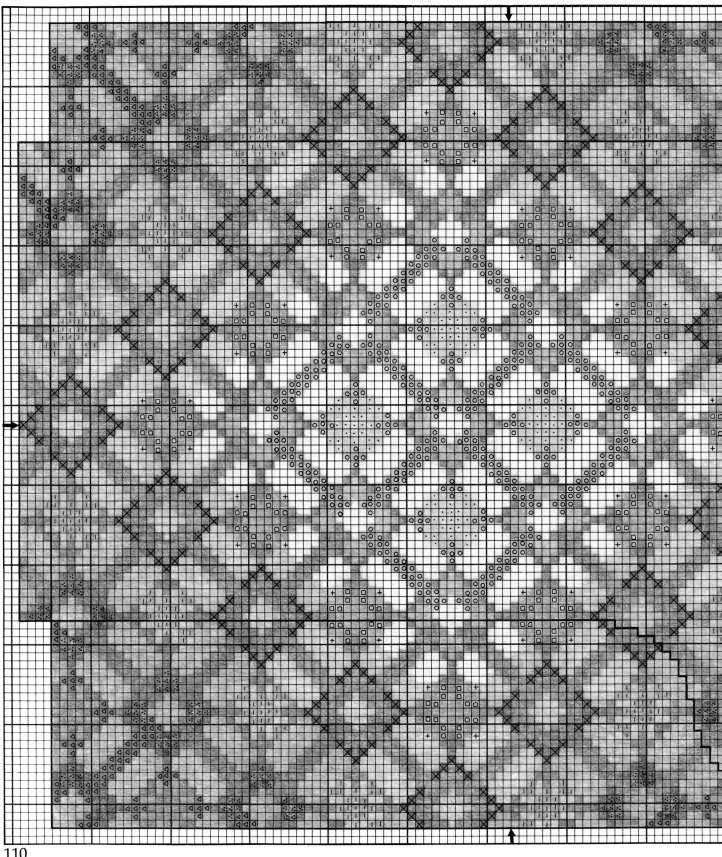

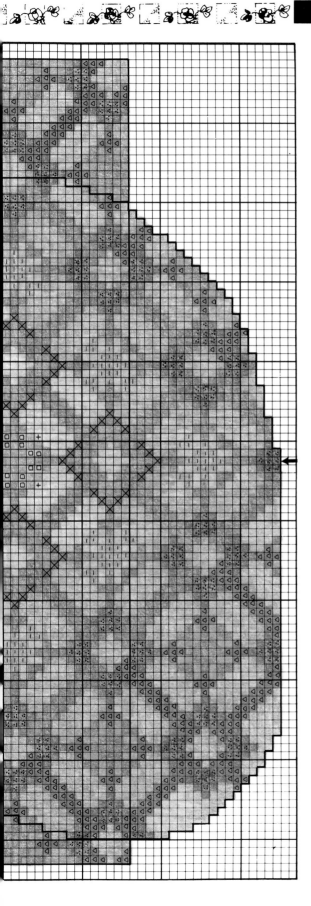

SAMPLE

The footstool is outlined in the graph of **Diamonds in a Dozen Colors**, pages 110 and 111. Stitched on White Hardanger 22 over two threads, the finished design size is 9⅛″ × 9⅛″. The fabric was cut 11″ × 11″. The stitch count is 101 × 101. Insert in footstool following manufacturer's instructions.

FABRIC	DESIGN SIZES
Aida 11	9⅛″ × 9⅛″
Aida 14	7¼″ × 7¼″
Aida 18	5⅝″ × 5⅝″
Hardanger 22	4⅝″ × 4⅝″

ANCHOR		DMC (used for sample)
		Step One: Cross-stitch (three strands)
300		745 Yellow-lt. pale
301	+	744 Yellow-pale
891		676 Old Gold-lt.
50	·	605 Cranberry-vy. lt.
75		604 Cranberry-lt.
66	−	3688 Mauve-med.
69		3687 Mauve
108		211 Lavender-lt.
104		210 Lavender-med.
105		209 Lavender-dk.
98		553 Violet-med.
99	✕	552 Violet-dk.
101		550 Violet-vy. dk.
118		340 Blue Violet-med.
119	△	333 Blue Violet-dk.
158		775 Baby Blue-lt. (one strand)
159		3325 Baby Blue (one strand)
128	○	800 Delft-pale
130		809 Delft
206		955 Nile Green-lt.
208	▫	563 Jade-lt.
187		992 Aquamarine

Step Two: Blending

187		992 Aquamarine (two strands)
189		991 Aquamarine-dk. (one strand)

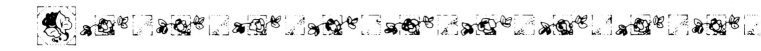

SAMPLE - VARIEGATED STOCKING

The stocking pattern is outlined in the graph of **Diamonds in a Dozen Colors**, pages 110 and 111. Stitched on White Hardanger 22 over two threads, the finished design size is 7½″ × 11¼″. The fabric was cut 9″ × 13″. The stitch count is 83 × 124.

SAMPLE - CUFFED STOCKING

The cuff is taken from the stocking pattern outlined in the graph of **Diamonds in a Dozen Colors**, page 110 and 111. Stitched on White Hardanger 22 over two threads, the finished design size is 5½″ × 2¾″. The fabric was cut 9″ × 9″. The stitch count is 60 × 30. Begin stitching at the top of stocking pattern graph, working down to complete 2¾″ of the design for the cuff.

112

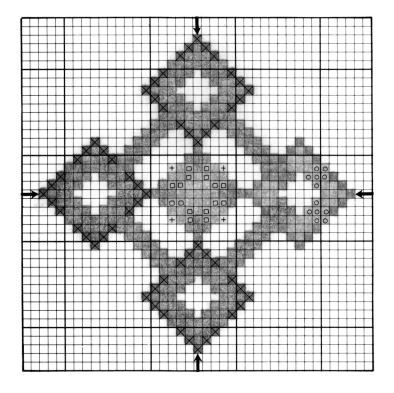

THREE ORNAMENTS

MATERIALS (for one)
Completed cross-stitch on white Aida 14 (see sample information); matching thread
Stuffing
1 yard of ⅛"-wide blue satin ribbon
1 yard of ⅛"-wide lavender satin ribbon
1 yard of ⅛"-wide turquoise satin ribbon

DIRECTIONS
All seam allowances are ¼".

1. For large ornament, cut fabric 6" square with design centered. Cut fabric 5" square for small ornament.

2. Fold under ¼" on all edges; baste.

3. With right side out, bring together two corners from same edge (see diagram). Slipstitch seam.

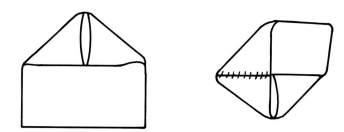

Repeat with third corner (see diagram). Fold and slipstitch fourth corner and third seam. Stuff ornament. Slipstitch fourth seam.

4. Handling all ribbon lengths as a single unit, tie into bow. Trim ends at irregular lengths.

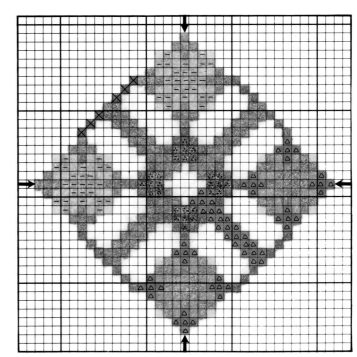

SAMPLE - SMALL ORNAMENT

Stitched on White Aida 14 over one thread, the finished design size is 2⅝″ × 2⅝″. The fabric was cut 6″ × 6″. The stitch count is 37 × 37.

SAMPLE - LARGE ORNAMENT

Stitched on White Aida 14 over one thread, the finished design size is 3⅜″ × 3⅜″. The fabric was cut 7″ × 7″. The stitch count is 47 × 47.

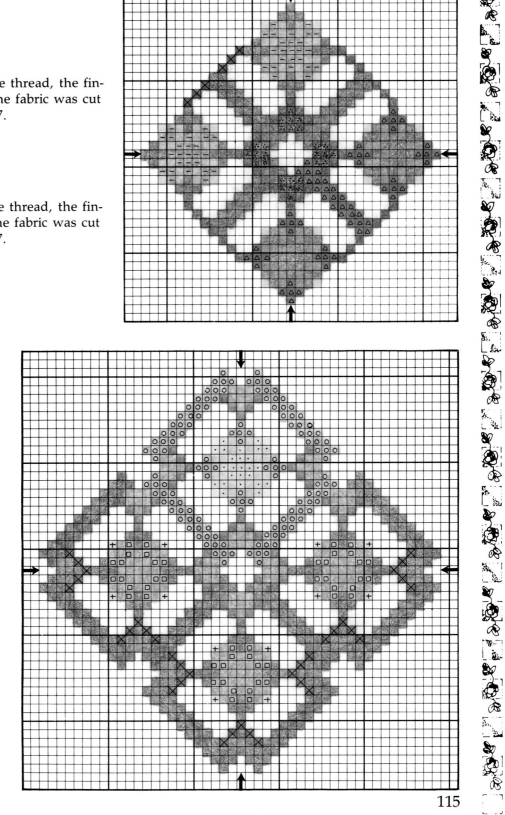

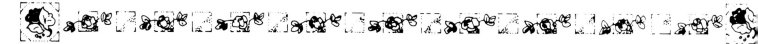

TWO JEWELED STOCKINGS

VARIEGATED STOCKING

MATERIALS

Completed cross-stitch on white Hardanger 22 (see sample information)
⅜ yard of lavender fabric; matching thread
2½ yards of variegated chiffon ribbon
1¼ yards of ⅝"-wide variegated purple-to-pink ribbon
1 yard of ⅛"-wide lavender satin ribbon
1 yard of ¼"-wide lavender silk ribbon
1⅛ yards of small cording
Tracing paper for pattern

DIRECTIONS

All seam allowances are ¼".

1. To make pattern, trace outline for stocking from graph on pages 110–111. Round off the heel and toe. Add ¼" seam allowance to all edges.
2. Cut three stocking pieces from lavender fabric. Cut one 1" × 3" piece for loop. Also cut 1¼"-wide bias, piecing as needed, to equal 1⅛ yards. Make 1⅛ yards of cording.
3. Stitch cording to right side of stitched stocking along sides and bottom. With right sides of one lavender stocking and stitched stocking together, stitch on stitching line of cording. Clip curved seam allowance. Turn.
4. Stitch cording around the top edge of stocking.
5. Stitch two remaining stocking pieces together for lining, leaving small opening in seam above heel.
6. Fold loop piece to measure ½" × 3". Stitch long edge. Trim seam allowance to ⅛". Turn. Fold to make 1½" loop. Pin raw ends of loop to right side seam.
7. Slide lining over stocking, right sides together and matching side seams. Stitch around top on stitching line of cording. Turn stocking through opening in lining. Slipstitch opening closed. Fold lining inside stocking.
8. Cut chiffon ribbon into two equal lengths. Match centers of all ribbon lengths. Handling all lengths as a single unit, tie into bow. Trim ends at irregular lengths.

CUFFED STOCKING

MATERIALS

Completed cross-stitch on white Hardanger (see sample information)
One 6" × 5½" piece unstitched Hardanger; matching thread
⅜ yard of lavender fabric; matching thread
¼ yard of white fabric
1 yard of variegated chiffon ribbon
1 yard of ¼"-wide lavender silk ribbon
1 yard of ⅜"-wide purple satin ribbon
1 yard of ⅛"-wide turquoise satin ribbon
1 yard of 1/16"-wide teal satin ribbon
Tracing paper for pattern
⅞ yard of small cording

DIRECTIONS

All seam allowances are ¼".

1. Complete Step 1 of Variegated Stocking.
2. For cuff, cut stitched piece 6" × 5½" with stitching across top 6" edge. Cut four lavender stockings. Also cut one 1" × 3" piece for loop. From white fabric, cut 1½"-wide bias, piecing as needed, to equal 32". Make 32" of cording.
3. Stitch cording to right side of one lavender stocking. Right sides of stocking piece with cording and second stocking piece together, stitch on stitching line of cording. Clip curved seam allowance. Turn.
4. Place two cuff pieces together. Stitch both 5½" edges. Fold right side out to measure 2¾" wide. Slide cuff over top edge of stocking, matching seams to side seams of stocking and all raw edges. Stitch cuff to stocking.
5. Stitch two remaining stocking pieces together for lining, leaving small opening in seam above heel.
6. Fold loop piece to measure ½" × 3". Stitch long edge. Trim seam allowance to ⅛". Turn. fold to make 1½" loop. Pin raw ends of loop to right side seam.
7. Slide lining over stocking, right sides together and matching side seams. Stitch around top through all layers. Turn stocking through opening in lining. Slipstitch opening closed. Fold lining inside stocking.
8. Match centers of all ribbon lengths. Handling all lengths as a single unit, tie into bow. Trim ends at irregular lengths.

A DAZZLING FOOT STOOL

MATERIALS

Completed cross-stitch on white Hardanger 22
⅜ yard of light blue fabric; matching thread
1⅛ yards of small cording
One 12″ × 12″ piece of muslin
Staple gun

DIRECTIONS

All seam allowances are ¼″.

1. Trim Hardanger ¼″ outside stitched design.

2. Cut four 2½″ × 13½″ strips from blue fabric. Also cut a 1½″–wide bias, piecing as needed, to equal 1⅛ yards. Make 1⅛ yards of cording.

3. Stitch cording to the right side of design piece.

4. Mark the center of one long edge of each blue strip. Also mark the center of each edge of stitched piece. Match centers of one long strip and one edge of design piece. Sew strip to design piece, stitching to within ¼″ of each corner; backstitch. Press seams toward the border.

5. To miter the corners, fold the right sides of two adjacent strips together and stitch at a 45-degree angle (see diagram). Trim the seam allowance to ¼″ and press. Repeat for each corner.

6. Center design piece over footstool top, matching corner seams to corners of top. Staple center of one edge to back, then to edge opposite first staple, pulling the fabric smooth. Repeat for centers of two remaining sides. Continue to staple one side and then the opposite side. Make corners as smooth as possible.

7. Fold under 1″ on edges of muslin piece. Staple to the back of the footstool top to hide the raw edges.

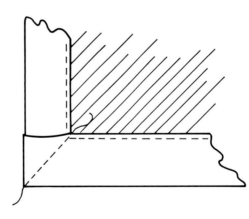

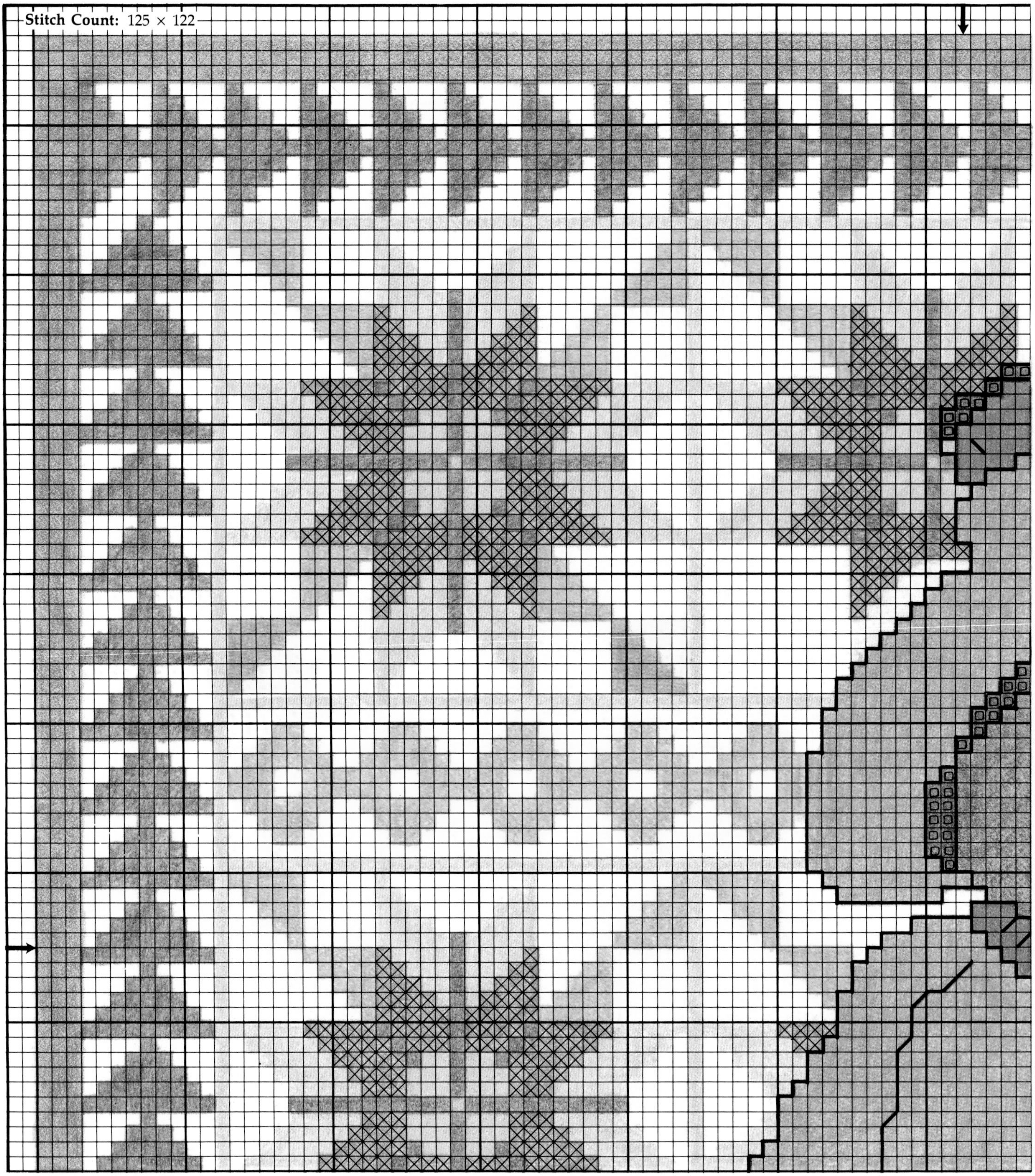
Stitch Count: 125 × 122

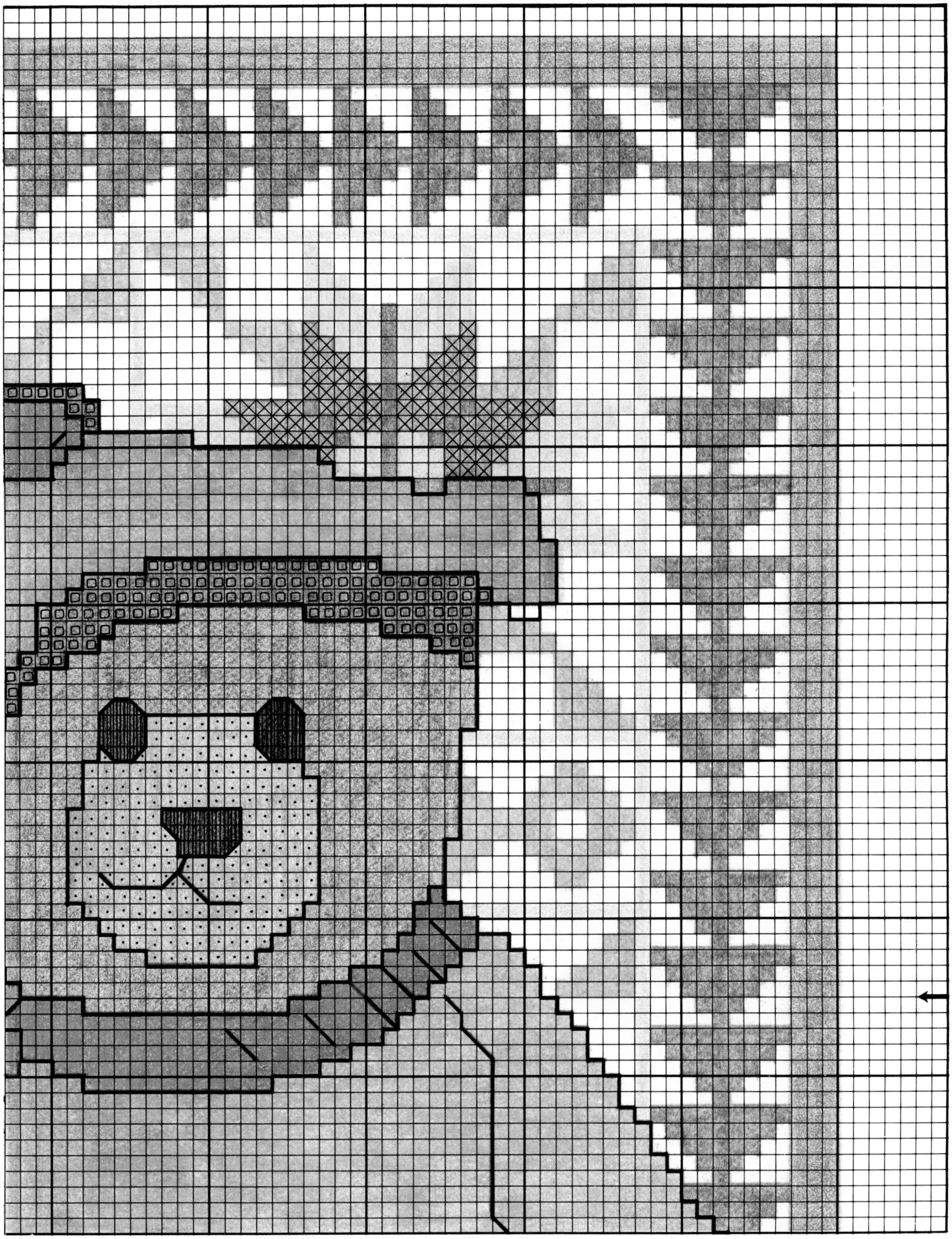

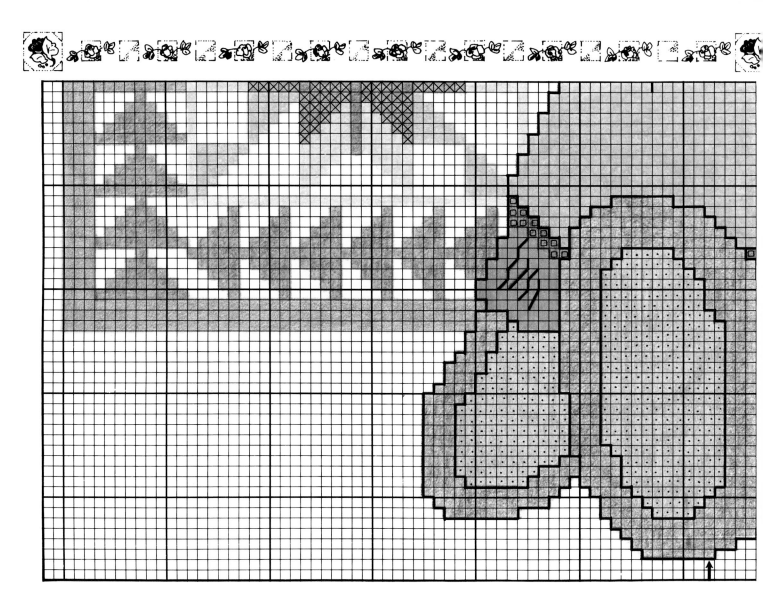

SAMPLE

Stitched on Floba 25 over two threads, the finished design size is 10″ × 9¾″. The fabric was cut 16″ × 16″.

FABRIC	DESIGN SIZES
Aida 11	11⅜″ × 11⅛″
Aida 14	8⅞″ × 8¾″
Aida 18	7″ × 6¾″
Hardanger 22	5⅝″ × 5½″

ANCHOR   DMC (used for sample)

Step One: Cross-stitch (two strands)

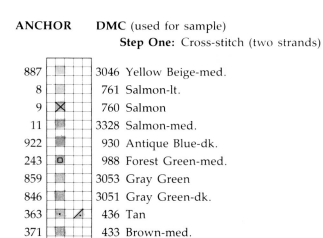

ANCHOR		DMC	
887		3046	Yellow Beige-med.
8		761	Salmon-lt.
9	✕	760	Salmon
11		3328	Salmon-med.
922		930	Antique Blue-dk.
243	⬜	988	Forest Green-med.
859		3053	Gray Green
846		3051	Gray Green-dk.
363	· ╱	436	Tan
371		433	Brown-med.

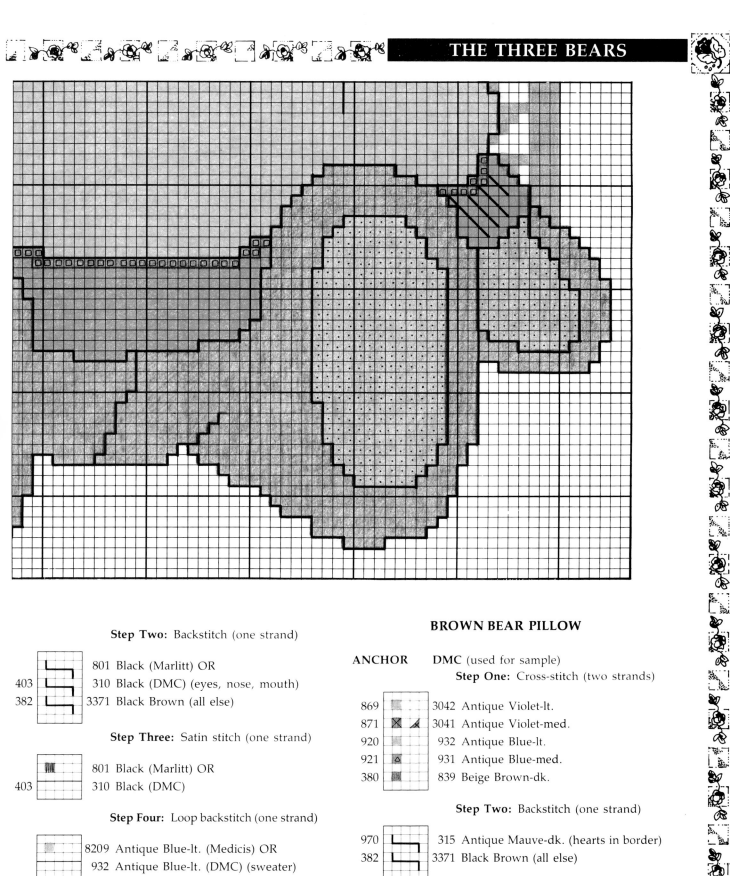

Step Two: Backstitch (one strand)

		801 Black (Marlitt) OR
403		310 Black (DMC) (eyes, nose, mouth)
382		3371 Black Brown (all else)

Step Three: Satin stitch (one strand)

		801 Black (Marlitt) OR
403		310 Black (DMC)

Step Four: Loop backstitch (one strand)

8209 Antique Blue-lt. (Medicis) OR
932 Antique Blue-lt. (DMC) (sweater)

BROWN BEAR PILLOW

ANCHOR		DMC (used for sample)

Step One: Cross-stitch (two strands)

869		3042 Antique Violet-lt.
871	✗ ⁄	3041 Antique Violet-med.
920		932 Antique Blue-lt.
921	△	931 Antique Blue-med.
380		839 Beige Brown-dk.

Step Two: Backstitch (one strand)

970		315 Antique Mauve-dk. (hearts in border)
382		3371 Black Brown (all else)

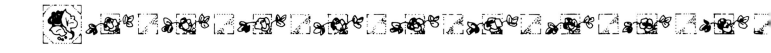

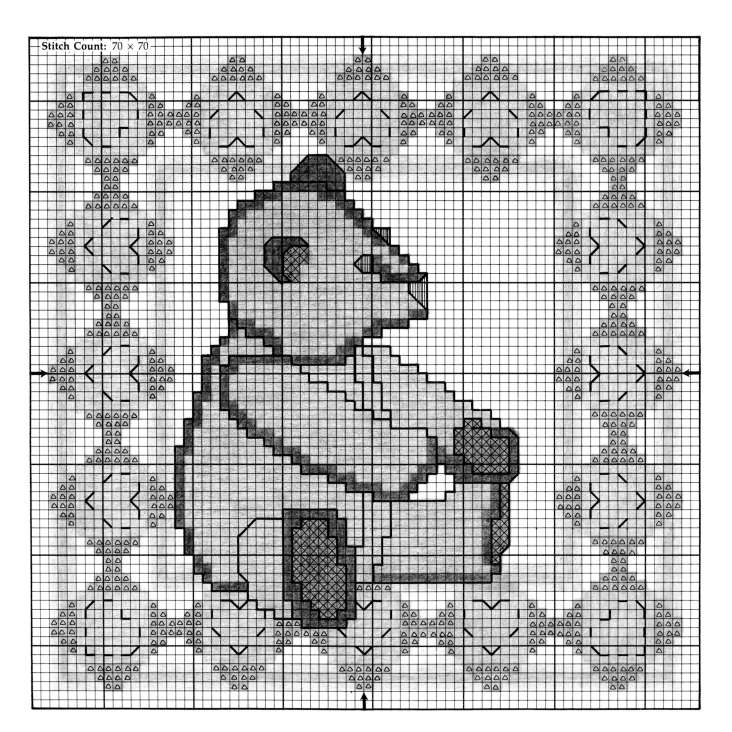

Stitch Count: 70 × 70

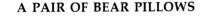

Step Three: Satin Stitch (one strand)

403	801 Black (Marlitt) OR 310 Black (DMC)

Step Four: Loop Stitch (one strand)

378	8501 Beige Brown-lt. (Medicis) OR 841 Beige Brown-lt. (DMC)

GRAY BEAR PILLOW

ANCHOR		DMC (used for sample)

Step One: Cross-stitch (two strands)

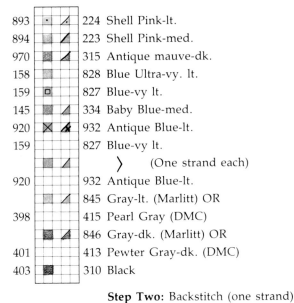

893	224 Shell Pink-lt.
894	223 Shell Pink-med.
970	315 Antique mauve-dk.
158	828 Blue Ultra-vy. lt.
159	827 Blue-vy lt.
145	334 Baby Blue-med.
920	932 Antique Blue-lt.
159	827 Blue-vy lt.
	⟩ (One strand each)
920	932 Antique Blue-lt.
	845 Gray-lt. (Marlitt) OR
398	415 Pearl Gray (DMC)
	846 Gray-dk. (Marlitt) OR
401	413 Pewter Gray-dk. (DMC)
403	310 Black

Step Two: Backstitch (one strand)

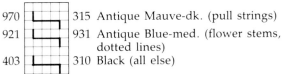

970	315 Antique Mauve-dk. (pull strings)
921	931 Antique Blue-med. (flower stems, dotted lines)
403	310 Black (all else)

Step Three: Satin stitch (one strand)

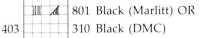

| 403 | 801 Black (Marlitt) OR
310 Black (DMC) |

A PAIR OF BEAR PILLOWS

SAMPLE

Stitched on Floba 25 over two threads, the finished design size is 5½″ × 5½″. The fabric was cut 14″ × 14″.

FABRIC	DESIGN SIZES
Aida 11	6⅜″ × 6⅜″
Aida 14	5″ × 5″
Aida 18	3⅞″ × 3⅞″
Hardanger 22	3⅛″ × 3⅛″

MATERIALS for one

Completed cross-stitch on Floba; matching thread
⅜ yard of unstitched Floba
¼ yard of blue or tan brushed nylon fabric; matching thread
⅛ yard of muslin fabric
⅛ yard of polyester fleece
2¼ yards of medium cording
One 12″ × 12″ pillow form
Dressmakers pen

DIRECTIONS

All seam allowances are ¼″.

1. Cut stitched Floba 10″ × 10″ with design centered. Cut one 10″ × 10″ piece from unstitched Floba for back. Cut one 2¾″ × 39″ strip of Floba for gusset.

2. Cut 1″-wide strip from brushed nylon piecing as needed, to equal 2¼ yards. Make 2¼ yards of cording to back piece.

3. Cut one 2¾″ × 39″ piece of muslin and one 2¾″ × 39″ piece of fleece.

4. Mark 1½″ intervals on right side of 2¾″ × 39″ Floba strip. Layer muslin, then fleece and Floba strip. Baste. Stitch on quilting lines.

5. Stitch cording to right side of design piece, clipping corners of seam allowance to turn corners. Stitch cording to for back piece.

6. Mark centers of both long edges of gusset. Measure 9½″ from centers and mark long edges. Pin marks to three corners of design piece with right sides together. Stitch on stitching line of cording, leaving fourth corner open. Measure exact fit of gusset. Stitch ends together. Complete stitching gusset to design piece.

7. Pin marks and seam to corners of back piece. Stitch on stitching line of cording leaving a 6″ opening. Insert pillow form. Slipstitch opening closed.

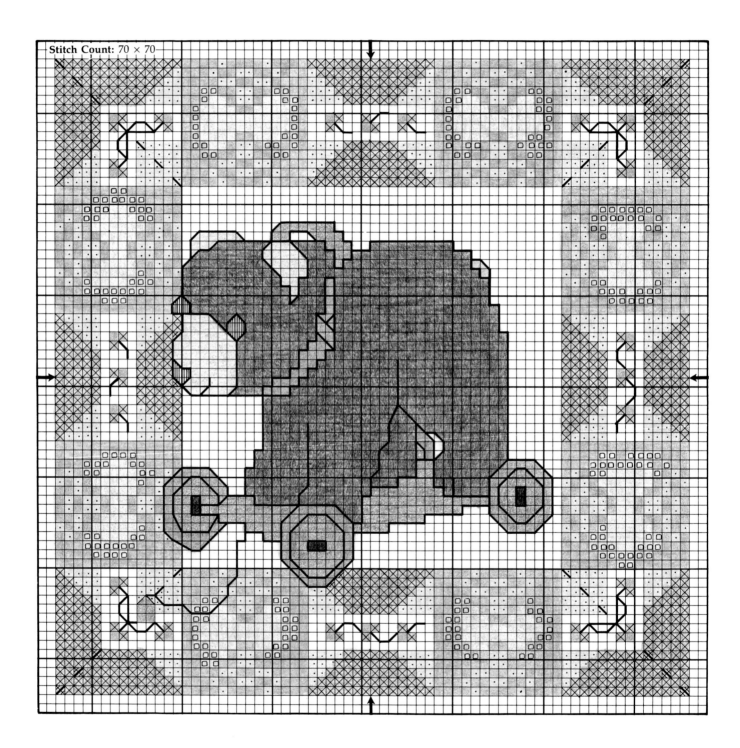

Stitch Count: 70 × 70

PORCELAIN DOLL BODY

MATERIALS

Porcelain doll parts
⅛ yard of white fabric; matching thread
Stuffing
Glue
Dressmaker's pen

DIRECTIONS

All seam allowances are ¼".

1. Cut out all body pieces according to patterns.

2. With right sides together, fold one arm piece and stitch along the outside edge, leaving the bottom edge open. Turn and stuff. At the opening, turn fabric under ¼". Insert a porcelain arm; glue. Repeat for second arm. Repeat for legs.

3. Sew darts in the body pieces. With right sides together, stitch front and back along the side edges of body piece, leaving 2" at top and entire bottom unstitched.

4. With the body piece wrong side out, place the legs inside the body so that the raw edges on the legs align with the raw edges on the bottom of the body. Sew across the bottom. Turn body right side out through top opening. Stuff. Slipstitch opening closed.

5. Tack the arms to the body at the shoulders. Glue the head to the top of the body.

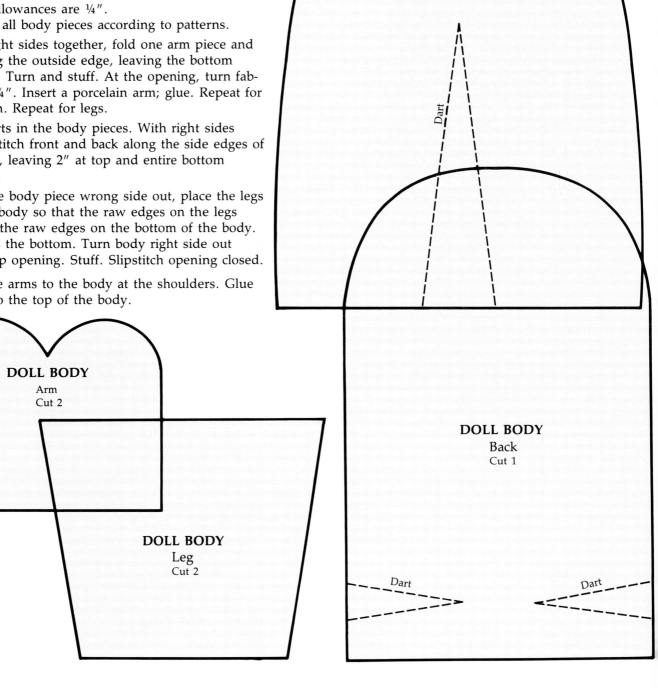

DOLL BODY
Front
Cut 1

Dart

DOLL BODY
Arm
Cut 2

DOLL BODY
Leg
Cut 2

DOLL BODY
Back
Cut 1

Dart

Dart

130

BASIC DRESS

MATERIALS

¼ yard of fabric; matching thread
Two small snaps
6"–8" of elastic thread
Dressmaker's pen

DIRECTIONS

All bodice seams are ⅛".

1. Cut one 6½" × 28" piece of fabric for the dress skirt. Cut the bodice front, bodice back and sleeves according to patterns.

2. With the right sides of one bodice front and two bodice back pieces together, stitch the shoulders. Repeat for the remaining bodice front and bodice back pieces.

3. Place right sides of the two bodices together, matching shoulder seams. Stitch along the center back, around the neck, and the second center back. Clip the curved edges. Turn right side out. Proceed to handle both layers of the bodice as one layer of fabric.

4. Stitch a narrow hem in the wrist edge of one sleeve. Stitch gathering threads in sleeve cap. Gather the sleeve to fit the armhole. Stitch the sleeve cap to the bodice. Repeat.

5. With right sides together, stitch one side seam and one sleeve. Repeat for the remaining side seam and sleeve. Sew elastic thread ¼" above the hem at the wrist, either by hand or with zigzag stitch over thread. Gather to fit the doll and secure.

6. Fold the skirt with right sides together and stitch the short ends together within 2" of the top edge; backstitch. (This seam is the center back; the long edge with the opening will be the waist.) Fold the edges of the opening double to the wrong side and stitch with a narrow hem.

7. Mark the center front of the skirt. Stitch gathering threads along the waist edge. Fold a ½" hem to the wrong side along the lower edge of the skirt. Stitch hem by hand or machine.

8. Mark the center front of the bodice at the waist. Gather the skirt to fit the bodice. Match the center of the skirt to the center of the bodice and stitch.

9. Sew snaps on the center back opening at neck and waist of dress.

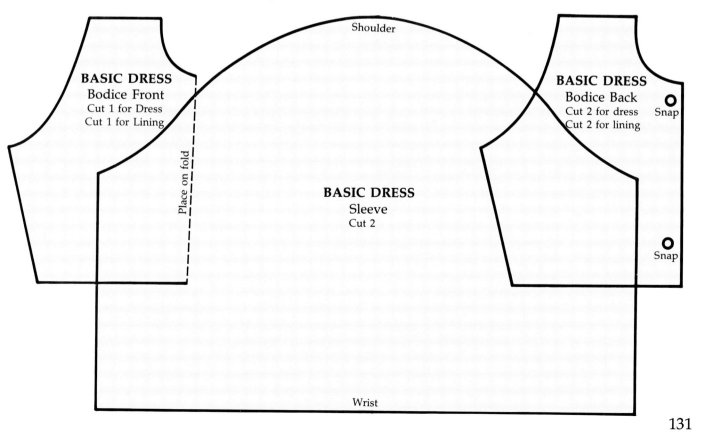

BASIC DRESS
Bodice Front
Cut 1 for Dress
Cut 1 for Lining

Place on fold

Shoulder

BASIC DRESS
Sleeve
Cut 2

Wrist

BASIC DRESS
Bodice Back
Cut 2 for dress
Cut 2 for lining

Snap

Snap

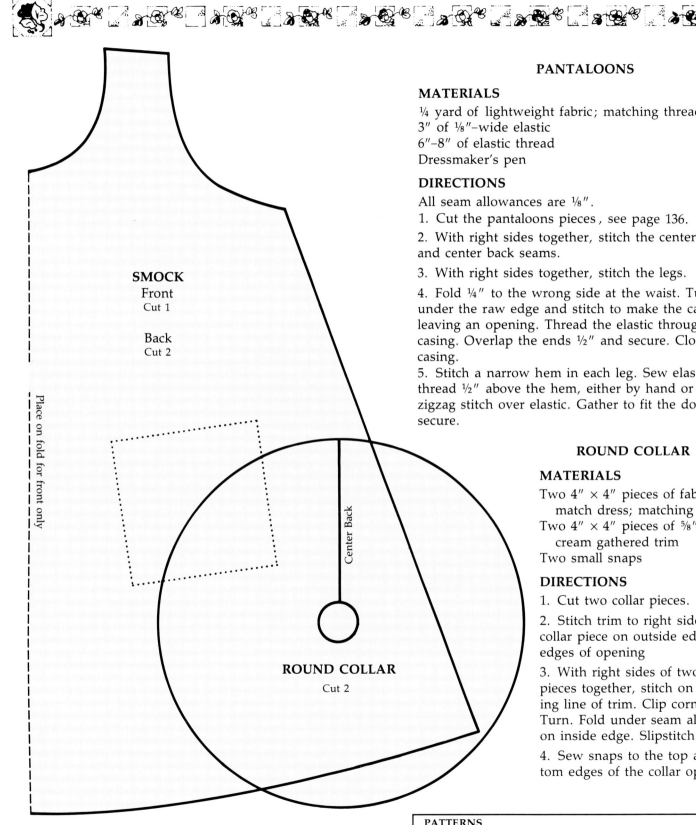

SMOCK
Front
Cut 1

Back
Cut 2

Place on fold for front only

Center Back

ROUND COLLAR
Cut 2

PANTALOONS

MATERIALS
¼ yard of lightweight fabric; matching thread
3″ of ⅛″–wide elastic
6″–8″ of elastic thread
Dressmaker's pen

DIRECTIONS
All seam allowances are ⅛″.

1. Cut the pantaloons pieces, see page 136.

2. With right sides together, stitch the center front and center back seams.

3. With right sides together, stitch the legs.

4. Fold ¼″ to the wrong side at the waist. Turn under the raw edge and stitch to make the casing, leaving an opening. Thread the elastic through the casing. Overlap the ends ½″ and secure. Close the casing.

5. Stitch a narrow hem in each leg. Sew elastic thread ½″ above the hem, either by hand or with zigzag stitch over elastic. Gather to fit the doll and secure.

ROUND COLLAR

MATERIALS
Two 4″ × 4″ pieces of fabric to
    match dress; matching thread
Two 4″ × 4″ pieces of ⅝″–wide
    cream gathered trim
Two small snaps

DIRECTIONS
1. Cut two collar pieces.

2. Stitch trim to right side of one collar piece on outside edge and edges of opening

3. With right sides of two collar pieces together, stitch on stitching line of trim. Clip corners. Turn. Fold under seam allowance on inside edge. Slipstitch.

4. Sew snaps to the top and bottom edges of the collar opening.

> **PATTERNS**
> Use tracing paper to trace the patterns from this book. Transfer all information. All patterns include seam allowance.

length of bias. Stitch gathering threads around the neck. Gather to fit bias, placing all fullness near the center front. With right sides together, stitch bias around the neck. Fold double to the wrong side and slipstitch.

3. With right sides together, stitch bias to armholes. Fold double to wrong side and slipstitch. With right sides together, stitch the side seams, securing bias ends in seam.

4. Zig-zag one edge of pocket piece. Fold under the remaining three edges ¼", then fold under the zig-zagged edge. (This is the top of the pocket). Pin pocket to the smock. Topstitch sides and bottom of the pocket.

5. Place gathered edge of the trim over the bottom edge of the smock. Stitch together and zig-zag the edge. Turn under ¼" hem and slipstitch.

6. Fold under the raw edges at the center back and hem. Sew the snap to the neck as the center back.

SAMPLE - ANNIE IN HER SMOCK

Both pieces use the same design taken from a **Sampler of Quilts**, page 7. Stitched with Mono Canvas 20 over one thread on cream fabric, the finished design size is 1" × 1". The canvas was cut 3" × 3". The fabric was cut 4" × 4". Her **Basic Dress** is green calico with the **Round Collar**. Both the collar and apron sport the same trim. The stitch count is 20 × 20. To stitch Annie's Purse, follow the instructions above for the pocket of Annie's Smock except cut the fabric 4" × 7". Center the design in the top half of the fabric.

MATERIALS for one smock

¼ yard of cream fabric (includes cross-stitched piece for pocket) see sample information; matching thread
½ yard of ⅝"–wide cream gathered trim to match trim on collar
One small snap

DIRECTIONS

All seam allowances are ¼".

1. Cut the smock front and back according to the patterns. Cut the design piece 2¼" square with the design centered. Also cut a 1"–wide bias, piecing as needed, to equal 18".

2. Stitch shoulder seams together. Cut one 5½"

MATERIALS for one purse

Completed cross-stitch on cream fabric for purse (see sample information); matching thread
½ yard of ¹⁄₁₆"–wide pink rayon braid

DIRECTIONS

All seam allowances are ¼".

1. Cut fabric 5½" × 2¾" with the top edge of the design 1⅛" from the top 2¾ edge and centered horizontally. Fold with right sides together to measure 2¾" × 2¾".

2. Stitch side seams.

3. To make the casing, fold ½" to wrong side around the top edge. Fold under ⅛" at raw edge. Stitch close to both folded edges. Turn.

4. Cut threads in side seam between rows for casing. Cut braid into two equal lengths. Thread through one opening and around casing, exiting from same opening. Knot ends. Repeat with the second length in the second opening.

WASTE CANVAS

Cut the waste canvas 1" larger on all sides than the finished design size. Baste the waste canvas to the fabric to be stitched. Complete the stitching. When stitching is complete, dampen the stitched area with cold water. Pull the waste canvas threads out one at a time with tweezers. It is easier to pull all the threads running in one direction first, then pull out the opposite threads. Allow the stitching to dry; then place face down on a towel and iron.

SAMPLE - ANNIE IN HER APRON

Annie is party-pretty in her cross-stitched apron. The basket design is one motif in **The Neighborhood**, page 17. Stitched on light gray Jobelan 28 over two threads, the finished design size for one motif is 2¼″ × 1¾″. The fabric was cut 24″ × 7″. Center and stitch the first motif 1½″ above the bottom 24″ edge. Repeat around apron leaving three stitches between motifs. Her **Basic Dress** is burgundy and she wears an eyelet **Petticoat** and white **Pantaloons**. The stitch count for one motif is 31 × 25.

GRAY APRON

MATERIALS

¼ yard of Light Gray Jobelan 28 (includes cross-stitched piece for skirt) see sample information; matching thread
One small snap

DIRECTIONS

All seam allowances are ¼″.

1. Trim apron skirt piece to 5½″ × 23″ with the bottom of the design 1″ above the lower edge. Draw the following pieces on the unstitched fabric, noting the grainline of the fabric:

> One 1″ × 9½″ for straps
> One 1″ × 18″ for ruffle
> Two ¾″ × 7½″ for waistband

Cut out each piece.

2. Fold the strap piece to measure ½″ × 9½″. Stitch the 8″ edge. Trim to ⅛″ seam allowance. Turn. Cut into two 4¾″ straps.

3. Place the right sides of the 5½″ ends together. Beginning at the cross-stitched edge, stitch together, leaving a 2½″ opening at the top edge; backstitch. (This seam is the center back.) Fold edge of opening to wrong side. Stitch around opening.

4. Zig-zag the ends and one long edge of the ruffle piece. Zig-zag the bottom edge of the skirt piece. Mark the centers of the raw edges of the ruffle and skirt pieces. Also mark the centers of the long edges of the waistband pieces. Stitch gathering threads on the raw edges of the ruffle and the skirt pieces.

5. Gather the ruffle to fit one long edge of one waistband piece, matching centers. Stitch together. With the right sides of the waistband and ruffle togehter, pin the second waistband over the first. Stitch both ends and the long edge where the ruffle is attached. Turn.

6. Gather the skirt to fit the second long edges of the waistband pieces, matching centers. Stitch together. Zig-zag the raw edges.

7. Attach the ends of the two straps ½″ either side of the center of the waistband. Place the apron on the doll and measure the length of the straps; pin. Secure ends of straps. Sew snap to waistband as center back.

SAMPLE - ANNIE IN HER LONG DRESS

Beautifully simple, Annie is ready for a seaside summer romance. The diamond shaped border design was inspired by **Three Maids A-Sailing**, page 26. Stitched on cream Hardanger 22 over one thread, the finished design size for one motif is ½″ × ½″. The fabric was cut 14″ × 30″. Stitch the border motif 1½″ above the bottom 30″ edge leaving three stitches between motifs. The stitch count for one motif is 11 × 11.

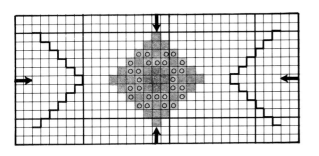

Step one: Cross-stitch (one strand)

869	o	3042 Antique Violet-lt.
871		3041 Antique Violet-med.
876		502 Blue Green

MATERIALS

⅜ yard of cream Hardanger 22 (includes cross-stitched piece for skirt); matching thread
One 4″ × 4″ piece of cream fabric for lining
⅞ yard of ⅛″–wide silver silk ribbon
Two small snaps
6″–8″ of elastic thread
Dressmaker's pen

DIRECTIONS

All bodice seams are ⅛″.

1. Cut one 13″ × 28″ piece of cream Hardanger for the dress skirt, positioning the bottom of the stitched design 1½″ above the bottom 28″ edge. Cut the bodice front, bodice back and sleeves according to patterns.

2. With the right sides of one bodice front and two bodice back pieces together, stitch the shoulders. Repeat for the remaining bodice front and bodice back lining pieces.

3. Place right sides of the two bodices together, matching shoulder seams. Stitch along the center back, around the neck, and the second center back. Clip the curved edges. Turn right side out. Proceed to handle both layers of the bodice as one layer of fabric.

4. Stitch a narrow hem in the wrist edge of one sleeve to finish edge. Stitch gathering threads in sleeve cap. Gather the sleeve to fit the armhole. Stitch the sleeve cap to the bodice. Repeat.

5. With right sides together, stitch one side seam and one sleeve. Repeat for the remaining side seam and sleeve. Sew elastic thread ¼″ above the hem at the wrist, either by hand or with zigzag stitch over thread. Gather to fit the doll and secure.

6. Fold the skirt with right sides together and stitch the short ends together within 2″ of the top edge; backstitch. (This seam is the center back; the long edge with the opening will be the waist.) Fold the edges of the opening double to the wrong side and stitch with a narrow hem.

7. Mark the center front of the skirt. Stitch gathering threads along the waist edge. Fold a ½″ hem to the wrong side along the lower edge of the skirt. Stitch hem by hand or machine.

8. Slipstitch ribbon to bottom edge of shirt ½″ above hem.

9. Sew snaps on the center back opening at the neck and 1″ below the neck.

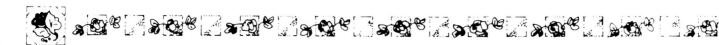

SAMPLE– ANNIE IN HER OVERALLS

Overalls, the perfect outfit for a spring planting day, show us a new side of Annie. The radish square design is taken from **A Rabbit in the Garden**, page 41. Stitched on white Belfast Linen 32 over two threads, the finished design is 1½″ × 1½″. The fabric was cut 4″ × 4″. The stitch count is 24 × 24.

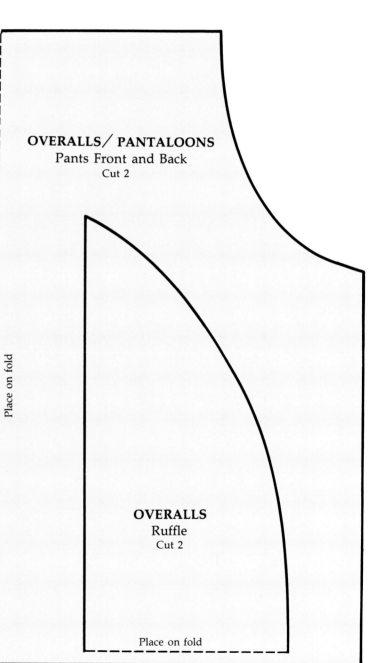

OVERALLS/ PANTALOONS
Pants Front and Back
Cut 2

Place on fold

OVERALLS
Ruffle
Cut 2

Place on fold

MATERIALS for blouse

⅛ yard of pink fabric; matching thread
Two small snaps
6″–8″ of elastic thread
Dressmaker's pen

DIRECTIONS

All seam allowances are ⅛″.

1. To make patterns for blouse, add 1″ to lower edge of bodice front and bodice back pieces of **Basic Dress** (page 131). Cut bodice front, bodice back and sleeve pieces according to patterns.

bodice back pieces together, stitch the shoulders. Repeat for the remaining bodice front and bodice back pieces.

3. Place right sides of the two bodices together, matching shoulder seams. Stitch along the center back, around the neck, and the second center back. Clip the curved edges. Turn right side out. Proceed to handle both layers of the bodice as one layer of fabric.

4. Stitch a narrow hem in the wrist edge of one sleeve. Stitch gathering threads in sleeve cap. Gather the sleeve to fit the armhole. Stitch the sleeve cap to the bodice. Repeat.

5. With right sides together, stitch one side seam and one sleeve. Repeat for the remaining side seam and sleeve. Sew elastic thread ¼″ above the hem at the wrist, either by hand or with zigzag stitch over thread. Gather to fit the doll and secure.

6. Sew snaps on the center back opening at the neck and 1″ below the neck.

MATERIALS for overalls

Completed cross-stitch on White Belfast Linen 32
¼ yard of light green fabric; matching thread
Three small snaps
6″–8″ of elastic thread
Dressmaker's pen

DIRECTIONS

All seam allowances are ¼″.

1. Cut completed cross-stitch piece ¼″ outside edges of stitching for bib. From green fabric, cut legs and ruffle according to patterns. Cut one piece of green fabric the same size as the design piece for the bib lining.

2. With right sides of design piece and lining together, stitch across the top edge. Fold right side out.

3. Sandwich bib between the right sides of two strap pieces aligned at the front end. Stitch entire long edge of strap. Repeat with additional strap pieces to form shoulder straps and waist.

4. Make a narrow hem in curved edge of ruffle pieces. Stitch gathering threads in straight edges of ruffle pieces. Gather ruffle pieces to 4½″. Place ruffle and shoulder strap with right sides together, placing ruffle ¼″ from front end of strap. Fold raw ends of ruffle and edges of strap ¼″ to the inside and slip-stitch. Repeat for other shoulder.

5. Mark centers of both long edges of remaining strips for waistband. With right sides together, sandwich bib between two waistband pieces, matching centers. Stitch one long edge and ends of waistband.

6. With right sides of leg pieces together, stitch the center front seam closed. Stitch the center back together within 2″ of the top edge. Fold the edges of the opening double to the wrong side and stitch with a narrow hem.

7. Place right sides together and stitch the inseam closed. Stitch gathering threads in waist. Turn. Gather to same size as waistband. Stitch together. Zig-zag over raw edges of all layers.

8. Stitch a narrow hem in each leg. Sew elastic thread ½″ above the hem, either by hand or with zigzag stitch over elastic. Gather to fit the doll and secure.

9. Sew snaps to each end of waistband.

SAMPLE - ANNIE IN HER CAPE

A trip to grandmother's house includes Annie's wonderful cape. The design is taken from a border in **Bouquets and Baskets**, page 53. Stitched on Victorian Christmas Green Lugana over one thread, the finished design for one motif is ⅜″ × ⅜″. Trace the cape front piece onto the green fabric twice. Match center block of graph to the center front ½″ from the straight edge. Repeat motifs both directions from center to fill 6″. The stitch count for one block is 8 × 8. Under her cape, Annie is wearing a pink calico **Basic Dress**, a pretty **petticoat** and matching **pantaloons**.

GREEN CAPE

MATERIALS

¼ yard of Victorian Christmas Green Lugana (includes cross-stitched piece for cape front pieces) see sample information; matching thread

¼ yard of dark green fabric for lining

½ yard of ¹/₁₆″–wide pink satin ribbon

DIRECTIONS

All seam allowances are ¼″.

1. Cut cape pieces from Lugana and lining.

2. Fold hood piece on center mark, right sides together. Stitch seam in center back. (See diagram.) Refold with center mark matching center back seam. Stitch the horizontal seam. (See diagram.) Repeat with hood lining.

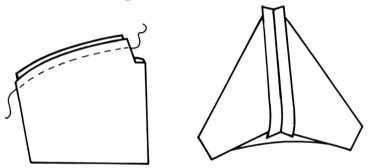

3. Stitch cape front pieces to cape back on side seams. Repeat for lining.

4. Mark center back of neckline. Match center back to seam in hood. Stitch hood to cape. Repeat for lining.

5. Match edges of cape and lining with right sides together. Stitch outside edges of cape, leaving a small opening in bottom edge. Clip corners. Turn. Slipstitch opening closed.

6. Cut ribbon into two equal lengths. Tack three small loops (see diagram) to seam joining hood and cape.

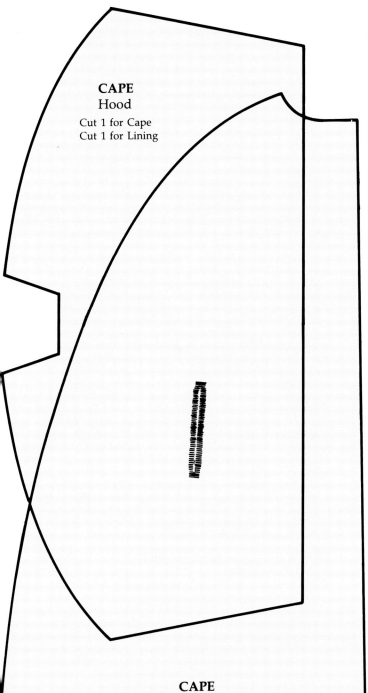

CAPE
Hood

Cut 1 for Cape
Cut 1 for Lining

CAPE
Front and Back

Cut 2 for Cape Front
Cut 1 on fold for Cape Back
Cut 2 for Cape Front Lining
Cut 1 on fold for Cape Back Lining

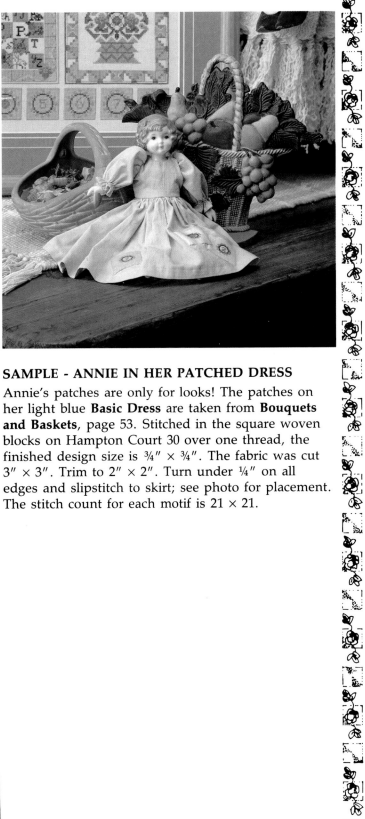

SAMPLE - ANNIE IN HER PATCHED DRESS

Annie's patches are only for looks! The patches on her light blue **Basic Dress** are taken from **Bouquets and Baskets**, page 53. Stitched in the square woven blocks on Hampton Court 30 over one thread, the finished design size is ¾″ × ¾″. The fabric was cut 3″ × 3″. Trim to 2″ × 2″. Turn under ¼″ on all edges and slipstitch to skirt; see photo for placement. The stitch count for each motif is 21 × 21.

EYELET PETTICOAT

MATERIALS

½ yard of 6″–wide eyelet; matching thread
3″ length of ⅛″-wide elastic

DIRECTIONS

1. Fold the eyelet or fabric with right sides together and stitch the 6″ ends.

2. If using fabric, stitch a narrow hem in one long edge; the eyelet will not need a hem.

3. Fold ¼″ to the wrong side at the waist. Turn under the raw edge and stitch to make the casing, leaving an opening. Thread the elastic through the casing. Overlap the ends ½″ and secure. Close the casing.

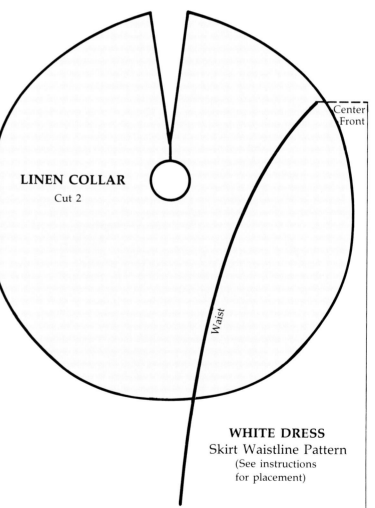

LINEN COLLAR
Cut 2

Center Front

Waist

WHITE DRESS
Skirt Waistline Pattern
(See instructions for placement)

SAMPLE - ANNIE IN HER LINEN COLLAR

Crisp and starched, Annie's linen collar dresses up her blue calico **Basic Dress**. The heart-shaped design is taken from **A Quilter's Prize**, page 73. Stitched on cream Belfast Linen 32 over two threads, the finished design size is 1¼″ × ¾″. The fabric was cut 6″ × 6″. Trace the collar pattern onto the Linen. Center the design in the front. The stitch count for the design is 19 × 13.

MATERIALS

Completed cross-stitch on cream Belfast Linen 32 (see sample information); matching thread
One 4″ × 4″ piece of cream fabric for lining
Two small snaps

DIRECTIONS

1. Place the collar pattern over the completed cross-stitch with design centered on bottom front of pattern. Trace and cut out the collar front.

2. Cut out the collar back from lining fabric according to pattern.

3. With right sides together, stitch around the outside edge, and ends. Clip corners. Turn. Fold under seam allowance on one inside edge. Slipstitch.

4. Sew snaps to the top and bottom edges of the collar.

SAMPLE - ANNIE IN HER WHITE DRESS

Annie's white dress is simple, elegant and suitable for any royal wardrobe. The design is taken from **The Princess and the Pea**, page 91. Stitched on Waste Canvas 20 over one thread, the finished design size is ⅝" × 2". The fabric was cut 4½" × 4½". The stitch count is 13 × 41.

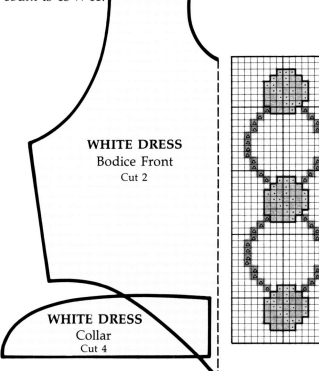

WHITE DRESS
Bodice Front
Cut 2

WHITE DRESS
Collar
Cut 4

MATERIALS

¼ yard of white fabric (includes cross-stitched piece for bodice); matching thread
Two small snaps
6"–8" of elastic thread
Dressmaker's pen

DIRECTIONS

All bodice seams are ⅛".

1. Cut one 6½" × 28" piece of fabric for the dress skirt. Fold skirt piece to measure 6½" × 14". (The fold is the center front.) Cut a V-shape in the center front according to pattern. Cut one Princess Dress bodice front with the cross-stitch design centered. Cut the second Princess Dress bodice front for lining and collar pieces according to pattern. From the **Basic Dress** (page 131), cut bodice back and sleeve according to pattern.

2. Stitch right sides of two collar pieces together along the end and curved edge. Clip corner. Turn. Repeat with the remaining two pieces.

3. Complete Step 2 of **Basic Dress**. Match collar pieces at center front and baste to the right side of bodice front with design. Complete Steps 3, 4, 5 and 6 of **Basic Dress**.

4. Fold a ½" hem to the wrong side of the skirt along the lower edge of the skirt. Stitch hem by hand or machine.

5. Stitch gathering threads along waist edge of skirt. Pin the deepest point of V-shape in skirt to point of bodice front. Gather the skirt to fit the bodice. Stitch together.

6. Sew snaps on the center back opening at the neck and waist of dress.

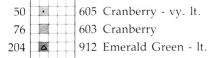

ANCHOR	DMC (used for sample)	
	Step One: Cross-stitch (one strand)	
50	605	Cranberry - vy. lt.
76	603	Cranberry
204	912	Emerald Green - lt.

Step Two: Backstitch (one strand)

76	603 Cranberry

SAMPLE—ANNIE IN HER ANGEL DRESS

Absolutely heavenly, Annie's dress has wings ready for flight. The design is taken from the **Small Ornament**, page 114. Stitched on White Linda 28 over two threads, the finished design size for one motif is 2⅝″ × 2⅝″. The fabric was cut 23″ × 7½″. The stitch count for one motif is 37 × 37. Begin stitching 3″ from 7½″ edge, and 2″ from bottom 23″ edge. Repeat motif eight times leaving no space between motifs.

MATERIALS

¼ yard of White Linda 28 (includes cross-stitched piece for skirt); matching thread
Small pieces of white fabric for bodice lining
¼ yard of ⅝″-wide variegated chiffon ribbon with gold metallic trim
¼ yard of 2″-wide white flat trim for wings
Four small snaps
6″–8″ of elastic thread
Dressmaker's pen

ANGEL DRESS
Hemline Pattern
(See instructions for placement)

DIRECTIONS

All bodice seams are ⅛″.

1. Cut one 22″ × 6¾″ piece from the cross-stitched piece for the dress skirt, positioning the bottom of the design 1″ above the bottom 22″ edge. From the remaining White Linda, cut a bodice front, bodice back and sleeves according to the **Basic Dress** pattern (page 131). From lining, cut bodice front and bodice back according to pattern.

2. Complete Steps 2,3,4,5 and 6 of **Basic Dress**.

3. Trace hemline pattern onto bottom edge of skirt placing points ½″ below the bottom point of the design. Adjust, if needed, to align the pattern and design especially at the center back.

4. Mark the center front of the skirt. Stitch gathering threads along the waist edge. Trim ⅜″ outside the marked hemline. Zig-zag the edge of the fabric. Fold to the wrong side on the hemline.

5. Complete Steps 8 and 9 of **Basic Dress**.

6. To make wings, stitch the ends of the flat trim together to make one continuous piece. Then place straight edges together, gathering fullness in ends as needed. Slipstitch straight edges together. Mark the center of the trim (see diagram). Sew a running stitch ¾″ from the center on either side of marked center;

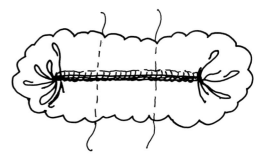

do not cut thread. Gather the trim to ½″ wide and secure thread (see diagram). On the wrong side of the wings, sew snaps at gathered sections. Mark placement for snaps on dress back. Sew snaps on the dress.

7. Cut the ribbon into two equal lengths. Tie around the waist of the dress.

INSTRUCTIONS

1. Find the center of the fabric. Zigzag the edges.

2. Cut the floss into 18″ lengths. Dampen and separate the strands. Put together the strands needed.

3. Locate the center of the design on the graph by following the vertical and horizontal arrows. Begin stitching at the center of the fabric. To make a waste knot, knot the floss and begin on the fabric front 1″ from the design area. Work several stitches over the thread to secure. Cut off the knot.

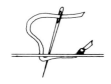

4. Make one cross for each symbol on the chart. For rows, stitch from left to right, then back. All stitches should lie in the same direction.

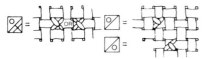

5. For half-crosses, make the longer stitch in the direction of the slanted line on the graph.

6. Backstitching is used to outline and accent. Use one strand less than for cross-stitch.

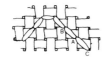

French Knot

Feather Stitch

Couch Stitch

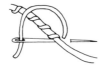

SUPPLIERS

All products are available retail from a merchant near you, or write the following suppliers:

Zweigart Fabrics:
Aida 14 (Cream, Natural, Light Blue)
Aida 18 (White)
Alice 27 (Green/White)
Belfast Linen (Cream, Driftwood, White)
Dublin 25 (Sand)
Floba 25
Hardanger 22 (White, Cream, Brown)
Linda 27 (White)
Lugana 25 (Victorian Christmas Green, Mushroom)
Mono Canvas 20
Waste Canvas 20
Zweigart/Joan Toggit Ltd., 35 Fairfield Place, West Caldwell, NJ 07006

Blue Glenshee Linen 29
Glenshee Egyptian Cotton Quality E 18
Anne Powell Heirloom Stitchery, P.O. Box 3060, Stuart, FL 33495

Hampton Square 30 - (Peach Blush, Cameo Rose, Lemon Cream)
Cross My Heart, Inc., 4725 Commercial Dr., Huntsville, AL 35816

Silk Canvas 30
Kreinik Manufacturing, P.O. Box 1966, Parkersburg, WV 26101

Jobelan (Cream, Ivory, Light Blue, Light Gray, Pewter)
Wichelt Imports, Inc., Rural Route 1, Stoddard, WI 54658

Beads
MPR Associates, P.O. Box 7343, High Point, NC 27264

Ribbon
C. M. Offray & Son, Route 24, Box 601, Chester NJ 07930-0601

Porcelain and Cut Crystal Jars
Anne Brinkley Designs, Inc., 21 Ransom Road, Newton Centre, MA 02159

Small Square Tables and Box Tables
Sudberry House, Box 895, Old Lyme, CN 06371

Porcelain Doll Parts
Chapelle Designers, Box 9252 Newgate Station, Ogden, UT 84403

Footstools
Sunshine Station, P.O. Drawer 2388, Hickory, NC 28603

Candlescreen
Plain 'n' Fancy, P.O. Box 357, Mathews, VA 23109

Bell Pull Hardware
Feldman Enterprises, 4215 Alta Vista Lane, Dallas, TX 75229

Oak Box
Reed Baxter Woodcrafts, Inc., P.O. Box 2186, Eugene, OR 97402

INDEX

For information on how you can
have *Better Homes & Gardens* magazine delivered to your door,
write to: ROBERT AUSTIN, P.O. BOX 4536, DES MOINES, IA 50336.